COLLABORATORS

A Play

JOHN MORTIMER

SAMUEL FRENCH

LONDON

NEW YORK   TORONTO   SYDNEY   HOLLYWOOD

MADE AND PRINTED IN GREAT BRITAIN BY
LATIMER TREND & COMPANY LTD PLYMOUTH

MADE IN ENGLAND

COLLABORATORS

First presented by Michael Codron Ltd.,
at the Duchess Theatre, London
on 18 April, 1973
with the following cast of characters:

Henry Winter	John Wood
Katherine Winter	Glenda Jackson
Sam Brown	Joss Ackland
Griselda Griffin	Gloria Connell

The play directed by	Eric Thompson
Setting by	Michael O'Flaherty

The action passes in the Winters' house in North-West
London

Time – the end of the 1950s

ACT I

Before and as the CURTAIN *rises we hear the sound of a record—a group singing in the manner of the late fifties*

Record "Sweet, sweet, the memories you gave me.
They're so sweet, the memories you gave me.
Take a fresh and tender kiss
And a stolen night of bliss,
One girl—one boy,
Two hearts—much joy.
Mem—oh—ries are made of this . . ."

The CURTAIN *rises on the living-room of a large Victorian house in North-West London at the end of the fifties. Finger-marked white paint, an electric fire with plastic coal, children's drawings and photographs pinned up. Posters for art exhibitions—"Matisse at the Tate", "Sculpture in Battersea Park". A door leads to the kitchen and a children's playroom. Back stage we can see the front door and stairs up to the bedrooms. A large table, on it a typewriter, paper, legal briefs, a dying pot plant, bills, empty bottles, children's clothes, etc., all in a mess. On the other side of the room a telephone on the floor beside the electric fire with the plastic coal. An old sofa. A radiogram which is playing*

Henry Winter comes in from the kitchen. He is in his thirties. He is carrying a white, elaborate new table lamp, with a base made from a pile of ceramic lemons, a contrast to the other rather old and battered furniture. He plugs it in. Turns off the other lights making the room look slightly more warm and romantic. He goes to a cupboard, finds one candlestick with a candle in it and puts it on the table. The record is still playing

Henry (*calling to someone in the kitchen next door*) When did we last have a dinner party?
Record "Add the wedding bells,
Two hearts—where love dwells,
Three little kids for the flavour . . ."
Henry (*stumbling over a small plastic fire-engine on the floor*) For the last ten years I seem to have lived entirely on nursery tea . . .
Record "Stir gently through the days,
See how the flavour stays,
Mem—oh—rees are made of this . . ."
Katherine (*calling from the kitchen*) Have you seen Suzannah's plastic knickers?

Record "Don't forget a small moonbeam,
Stir lightly with a dream.
One man—one wife,
Two hearts—through life,
Mem—oh—rees are made of this . . ."

Henry (*calling back*) No! (*He goes back to the cupboard, finds the other candlestick, broken*) You know what it's like? Living with children? It's like spending your days in a home for very old, incontinent Irish drunks! It's like life in a colony of hostile meths drinkers! They come swaying up to you with their dribble and their deep hoarse cries and you smile —a smile of propitiation—and then they take a great swipe and smash the other candlestick.

Henry puts the bits of broken candlestick back in the cupboard and goes out to the kitchen.
  Katherine comes in. She's the same age as her husband—very attractive although at the moment her head is turbaned in a towel. She wears trousers and smokes a lot. She carries a hairbrush. She stops the record-player and squats by the fire to brush her hair

Katherine I told you—I've lost Suzannah's plastic pants.
Henry (*off*) Thank God!
Katherine Why?
Henry I can't stand them, that's why.

Henry enters carrying an old Chianti bottle

Katherine You don't have anything to do with them.
Henry I see them in the distance. As they retreat I notice our children's bottoms swathed in pixie hoods. It's like an aerial view of American tourists in the rain. (*He fits another candle into the Chianti bottle and puts it on the table*) I think that looks pretty distinguished. (*He looks at the bookshelves anxiously*) The children are getting so tall. (*He takes out a book*) Someone's started to eat the pornography. (*He puts it in a higher shelf*) I got a new lamp fixed up. (*He moves the new lamp an inch or two, admires it*)
Katherine (*looking at the lamp*) Bloody Hollywood!
Henry What? (*He puts the typewriter on the sideboard and clears the table generally*)
Katherine Did you tell the bank manager you bought a bloody Hollywood lamp? He rang again today. (*In a Scots accent*) "Mr MacFeeling of the Westminster this end. Is your husband at home just now? The tide would appear to be going out on his overdraft." I'm sick of telling him— you're locked in the downstairs loo. Trembling!
Henry Why not tell him we've got to live? (*He goes to a cupboard, gets out paper table napkins and glasses, starts to lay the table*)
Katherine I did. He said that might not be necessary. Why can't you speak to him? I don't think the Westminster Bank believe I've *got* a husband!

Henry We've got great news for MacFeeling. It's going to be all right.

Katherine What?

Henry Mr Samuel Brown's going to solve . . . all our problems. (*He puts table napkins, neatly folded, into glasses. Three places*)

Katherine It's not tonight?

Henry (*looking at her*) You know damn well it's tonight. That's why you washed your hair—because someone's coming to dinner.

Katherine I washed my hair because no-one's coming to dinner.

Henry (*admiring the table*) What do you think it looks like?

Katherine Marvellous. Like New Year's Eve at the Rotary Club. Haven't we got any streamers?

Henry We don't need streamers. All we need is for you to be reasonably polite to Mr Brown. (*He lays plates, etc., for three places, then tidies the room generally during the following*)

Katherine No.

Henry What?

Katherine No. I don't think so really. I'd rather live with the overdraft.

Henry For God's sake! Why?

Katherine He'll—corrupt you.

Henry How on earth is he going to manage that?

Katherine (*standing and combing her hair, looking at her reflection in the glass*) If you let that Mr Brown in here, he will undoubtedly corrupt you. He wants to change you. I didn't marry a movie writer.

Henry You didn't marry me.

Katherine Oh, really?

Henry You married someone inexperienced and painfully thin. Who'd never heard of nappy rash or Volpar Jells or Castle Pudding or Farex or Groats or Acute Menstrual Depression. I was someone else entirely.

Katherine And now you'll be someone ghastly.

Henry *Who* do you think?

Katherine Someone who drives a white Jag and cashmere polo necks and an identity bracelet and a house in Weybridge . . .

Henry You think Sam Brown'll do that to me?

Katherine And two bloody Hollywood lamps. With a white leather sofa in between them. Full of Miss Rank-Odeon unzipping her plastic tiger-skin ski-pants. I want no part of it.

Henry He's not going to change my life.

Katherine No?

Henry He's harmless . . .

Katherine Really?

Henry As a matter of fact he's quite civilized. He's someone who listens to radio plays.

Katherine I don't believe it.

Henry Why?

Katherine There isn't anybody who listens to radio plays.

Henry That's why he rang up. He said he'd heard my play on his car radio. He was stuck in a traffic jam at Marble Arch . . .

Katherine (*incredulously*) For an hour!

Henry That's why he asked me to lunch.

Katherine You're a pushover!

Henry At the "Pastoria", Leicester Square.

Katherine And I bet you said "yes" after the *hors d'oeuvre*.

Henry I told you—he's putting together this little package.

Katherine You'll be in it!

Henry What?

Katherine Neatly wrapped in brown paper and tied up with string. Has he ever actually made a film?

Henry I think . . . just commercials so far.

Henry goes out of the door into the kitchen. She shouts to him there and he shouts back

Katherine Tell him you're a respectable lawyer! You don't want anything to do with his little packages.

Henry (*coming back into the room with a bottle of wine which he opens and then puts down by the electric fire*) I told you. He wants me to write something. That's all. About marriage. It's a subject he thinks might suit me.

Katherine Why?

Henry I'm married, aren't I? For God's sake! Why else am I living in a sea of plastic knickers?

Katherine Is that what you're going to write—a commercial—about our marriage?

Henry Sam Brown says the aim is to do something truthful.

Katherine shivers

What's the matter?

Katherine I'm afraid.

Henry Whatever of?

Katherine We've got too many weapons.

Henry You know, I haven't got the slightest idea what you're talking about.

Katherine The children. My mother and your mother. My past and your future—your car and my furniture. They're all like loaded guns we can pick up and use—if ever—if ever things get a little—out of control.

Henry If ever?

Katherine The shopping and the overdraft and the John Barnes account, all little hand grenades lying about the place . . . and you want to import a great thousand ton all purpose hydrogen bomb we can throw at each other the day you're feeling a little bored.

Henry (*lighting the candles*) Dramatize! Dramatize everything . . .

Katherine It's like standing on the edge of the sea . . .

Henry Doom! Doom! The Lady Macbeth of Belsize Park!

Katherine On the edge of the sea and you have an irresistible urge to walk in, until the water closes over your head.

Henry Ring the alarm bell! Lines of murdered children, stretching as far as the eye can reach ... It's nothing but a film producer coming for dinner!

Katherine My Aunt Freda drowned herself, in Prestatyn. The sea was very shallow—she was only a small woman but she had to walk out two miles until she could get her head under. I wonder what she thought about all the time she was walking ...

Henry (*going to the radiogram and putting on a record*) Will you stop acting!

Katherine What's your part, darling? Little orphan Annie—eagerly waiting for the rich squire to come in and seduce her? It's all laid on, isn't it? Music and candles—how disgusting!

The record starts to play. Elvis is singing

Henry starts to dance a slow 1950's jive. He puts out his hand for Katherine to dance with him. She shakes her head

Katherine I'm not dancing with you tonight. Anyway, it's not your period.

Henry What's my period?

Katherine I'd say late Carmen Miranda ...

Henry (*stopping dancing, angry, and moving to the kitchen door*) Try and not be brutal to Mr Brown.

Henry exits to the kitchen
    Katherine picks up the towel, puts it round her neck like a muffler, and also exits. The record goes on playing

Katherine returns with a large wooden clothes horse hung with nappies which she plumps down in front of the electric fire

The front doorbell rings

Katherine Oh, shit!

Katherine blows out the candles then runs off by the entrance leading to the staircase. She returns with a plastic baby bath full of washing and puts it on the table

The doorbell rings again. Katherine turns off the record, pushes the baby's potty down stage. The doorbell rings a third time. She goes and opens the front door

Sam Brown enters—it is difficult to tell his age—sometimes he seems gay and enthusiastic, at others haggard and middle-aged. He speaks with a variable American accent and is wearing an anonymous Brooks Brothers suit, a black knitted tie which he loosens at moments of stress and a small tartan trilby hat. He looks at the domestic chaos..

Katherine follows him into the room. A sound of chopping is heard from the kitchen

Sam Brown. Sam Brown. (*He takes off his hat*) You must be his wife.
Katherine (*whispers back*) Must I? That's depressing.
Sam Is it?
Katherine I always thought I exercised a vague kind of choice. I'm sorry about the muddle—kids. You know how it is.
Sam (*whispering*) No. No.
Katherine (*whispering*) What?
Sam I don't know.
Katherine (*looking at him*) You haven't got any?
Sam No. No. I haven't.
Katherine (*looking at him as though he were some rare phenomenon*) How extraordinary! (*Pause*) Why're we whispering?
Sam Your feller's at work. Isn't that the typewriter?
Katherine No. The chopper.

Sam looks at her, surprised

Sam The chopper?
Katherine He's doing his *Pot au feu*.
Sam Pardon me?
Katherine It's stew. He cuts recipes out of the *Evening Standard*.
Sam (*after a pause, looking at her, worried*) You mean, he cooks?
Katherine Practically the whole time.
Sam This man writes dramatic material for the radio and also cooks!
Katherine (*picking up baby clothes*) And dusts and sprays things with Gleam and arranges furniture and administers aspirin to wilting chrysanths.
Sam Jeezus!
Katherine He doesn't often change nappies or make beds or put washers on taps. That's my work.
Sam Kerist . . . !
Katherine Yes. (*She picks up the potty*) I was just going to settle the children.
Sam How many—exactly?
Katherine Does it matter?
Sam No—but . . .
Katherine More, probably, than you've ever seen in your life. Many, many more.
Sam Before you go . . . can I ask you something quite frankly? As Henry's wife? How's his availability?
Katherine His what?
Sam His availability. How is it?
Katherine Pretty good first thing in the morning. Not so marvellous last thing at night.
Sam I mean—is he really going to have time to take on this assignment?
Katherine (*decidedly*) No.
Sam What?
Katherine No. He's certainly not going to have time for that.

Katherine exits upstairs

Sam starts to examine the room curiously, as though it were a strange country

Henry enters carrying an empty casserole dish from which he is taking a pair of children's plastic pants

Henry Look, it's unbelievable! An incredible place to find them. (*He throws the pants down into the plastic bath, bangs the dish down on the table*) Oh, Mr Brown. You're here early.

Sam What a lovely home you have here.

Henry (*incredulously*) What?

Sam This certainly is a lovely home.

Henry You're joking?

Sam Dickensian!

Henry You can say that again.

Sam How would a person find—a truly Dickensian home such as this?

Henry Only by mistake. Have a drink? (*He goes to the bottle of wine by the fire*)

Sam Maybe later . . .

Henry (*pouring himself a glass and holding it up to the light*) Something shy and anonymous from the off licence . . .

Sam Mr Winter. May I call you Humphrey?

Henry If you like. My name's Henry actually.

Sam Henry. I'm Sam. And I have already met your lovely lady.

Henry Oh? (*He drinks quickly*)

Sam She let me into your front door and was gracious enough to engage me—in conversation.

Henry (*picking up the clothes horse and carrying it out*) She seems to have turned the place into a kind of steam laundry.

Sam Henry. Henry. I want you to tell me something.

Henry (*returning*) What? (*He picks up the plastic tub of washing, puts the saucepan on top of it*)

Sam The process of procreation and childbirth—it's not particularly difficult, is it?

Henry (*putting the dish into the plastic tub, and going out with it into the kitchen*) No.

Sam It doesn't call for any special skills or aptitude which I may not possess?

Henry (*coming back into the room*) I don't think so.

Sam Or demand arduous training or a long period of study?

Henry Certainly not. What's troubling you, Mr Brown?

Sam How come your wife made me feel so suddenly inadequate?

Henry Ah, well now . . . when you get to know her . . .

Sam Something of a ball cutter, is she, your good lady?

Henry Well now, Mr Brown.

Sam Sam. I'm Sam, Henry. Is she the sort that enjoys to cut ball occasionally? I feel we should be very frank with each other at the outset of what I hope will be a long and happy relationship.

Henry (*moving away from him*) I was just—chopping parsley.

Sam You are wandering from the point. Something here's a little painful for you to contemplate, is that it? Your lady does not feel that we should work together. She thinks that your schedule is such that you may be unavailable?

Henry What?

Sam She thinks you might have too much on your plate already.

Henry Too much on my plate? That's ridiculous. Look. Why don't you sit down, or play a record, or—something.

Henry moves towards the kitchen door. Sam follows and stands very close to him

Sam She also suggested you were cooking.

Henry Well, that's right. It's a kind of casserole, quite honestly. It won't take me a minute.

Sam Where I come from only faggots cook.

Henry (*looking at him, not knowing what to say*) Do they? Where is that exactly? I know. You told me . . .

Sam To cook is always thought of as the hallmark of a fag.

Pause. Henry can think of nothing to say

What was your wife doing, Henry—laying such emphasis on your cooking abilities? Was she trying to cut your balls off, feller?

The telephone rings

Henry Excuse me. (*He goes to the telephone*) Oh, hullo, Miss Griffin . . . Of course I don't mind you ringing me at home . . . No, I'm not busy, not really . . .

Sams picks a book from the shelf, is surprised

Oh . . . It's about our murder. Yes. How's it going?

Sam looks up from the book, more surprised

To be committed on Thursday? Well, that doesn't give us much time.

Sam puts down the book and moves closer to him

I mean attempted murder's not a thing we can rush into—that is, if I'm not going to make a complete and utter fool of myself.

Sam has now moved very close to Henry and is standing beside him as he talks to the phone

Look shall we talk about it tomorrow . . . ? Four-thirty. Fine. (*He scribbles a note on the pad by the phone*) We'll have tea in the Kardomah. (*He puts down the phone, finds he is looking into Sam's anxious face*)

Sam Murder? Did you say—attempt to murder?

Henry My first time, actually . . .

Katherine comes down the stairs

Katherine He's a lawyer. Hasn't he told you?

Henry A barrister.

Sam Henry! You have a barristership?

Katherine No-one gets told everything—about my husband. (*She pours herself a drink*) Have you told Mr Duffield you're writing a film about marriage, darling?

Sam Who's Mr Duffield?

Katherine He sits every night in the condemned cell, wondering how the show's going.

Henry Not the condemned cell. Brixton. The Hospital Wing. They get television and tranquillizers.

Katherine Just like us.

Henry I'm worried about Bernard Duffield, as a matter of fact. He seems to have a deep desire to be found guilty.

Katherine Then he's certainly picked the right barrister.

Sam makes a private cutting gesture with his hand to Henry

Care for a drink, Mr Brown?

Sam Scotch, please. On the rocks. I'm afraid my blood alcohol is sinking a little low.

Katherine (*pouring him a glass of wine*) I'm afraid we've got no rocks.

Sam Murder, uh? That must be interesting. Tell me . . .

Henry "How do you defend a person you think's really done it?"

Sam How did you know I'd ask you that?

Henry Everyone does. Well, the answer is—I just don't make up my mind.

Katherine He finds that perfectly easy. Not making up his mind comes quite naturally to Henry.

Henry It's just a question of suspending belief . . .

Katherine That was his belief you passed in the hall, it's been hanging up there for years!

Sam I guess the movie business calls for a little more sincerity.

Katherine Sincerity? We must get some of that in for the next time you call. (*To Henry*) Write it on the blackboard, darling. (*To Sam*) He has a little blackboard in the kitchen. He writes down things he's short of. Garlic, sweet and sour sauce, sincerity . . .

Sam (*very seriously*) Add one more quality, Katherine.

Katherine What?

Sam Hard work. It's pretty ruthless. The Show Business.

Katherine You'll find murder gentle by comparison?

Sam You go to Honolulu at all?

Katherine Not regularly.

Sam Katherine, let me tell you something. The brain of a dolphin is half as big again as the brain of man!

Katherine No kidding!

Sam They have this great Dolphinarium in Honolulu. And you should see these fish perform! Better than actors. They solve mathematical problems. They dance the—Da Da Da Da Pom—you know!

Katherine (*helpful*) The Skaters' Waltz.

Sam Yes. Well, in the hotel there the Maître D offered me "Mai Mai steak". Very good. Natural, sustaining and delicious food. Until I asked what was "Mai Mai" exactly. You know what they told me?

Katherine You were eating those unfortunate dolphins that couldn't do Strauss waltzes?

Sam Right! She's right! Kinda frightening, though, isn't it?

Henry (*refilling Sam's glass*) Is it?

Katherine Oh, Henry's not frightened. He'll whistle and ring bells and dance the waltz even if there's no water in the tank. I'll get the stew . . .

Katherine goes into the kitchen, banging the door after her

Sam is left looking at Henry. Henry brings down his own chair and sets it at the table

Sam Know what I told you, feller? (*He drinks*) Professionally. A modern marriage. What a great story.

Katherine enters with a casserole and plates, which she puts on the table

The three sit to eat, Sam in the middle

The Lights fade, then come up as before. Dinner is over. Sam is explaining to Katherine

I tell you this group—this group I've done commercials for—they've become so big in footwear they're investing in talent . . . ! They want to make something really interesting. (*He yawns*)

Katherine About marriage?

Sam They figure—a subject that concerns everyone . . .

Katherine Like feet . . .

Sam I believe—if we can put a script together that they go for—they'll find us finance, Henry. No question. It will be found eventually . . .

Henry Well, finance would certainly come in useful.

Katherine (*to Sam*) I thought you wanted *him* to do it.

Sam What?

Katherine I thought Henry was going to put the script together . . .

Sam We'll work together, won't we, feller? Knowing each other as we do —we'll work together as a team. It's a challenge!

Henry (*unenthusiastically*) Yes. I suppose it is.

Sam It's not going to be easy. I'm not going to kid you about that. We'll have our bad moments, sure. We'll cry together, but have our laughs also, let's hope. (*He gets up*) Well, you lovely people. It was a pleasure and a privilege to enter your home. (*He punches Henry lightly on the shoulder*) Great stew. You did a great job.

Katherine He'll make a lovely wife. (*She moves away from them, pours herself a glass of wine*)

Sam (*looking after her*) What a subject! (*He moves with Henry towards the front door*) Ring me next week, uh?

Sam goes

As Sam exits, Katherine starts to laugh. Henry sees her, pushes the front door. It does not shut. Henry goes towards Katherine and puts his arm round her. They both laugh.

Henry Cry together! Do you think we have to?

Katherine What did he propose to you at lunch, actually? Sounds to me as if he proposed marriage. (*She stops laughing*) He's ruthless! (*She moves away from him*)

Henry Probably.

Katherine Russian, of course.

Henry He's not Russian!

Katherine What is he then?

Henry I believe he was born in a small office off Wardour Street.

Katherine With an American accent!

Henry They learn that. In the Berlitz School, Tottenham Court Road. Anyway, why should an American accent make him Russian? (*He drains the wine bottle into his glass, drinks*)

Katherine That's his cunning.

Henry Oh, yes?

Katherine You can't believe a word he says.

Henry That's true.

Katherine Pretending to be a film producer!

Henry People who pretend to be film producers *become* film producers. It's the only way.

Katherine Modern marriage! What a ridiculous idea!

Henry Exactly. If people want marriage they can do it quietly amongst themselves. They don't need to go out and watch other people at it.

Katherine Did you tell him that?

Henry Of course I did. Didn't you hear me?

Katherine You kissed his arse!

Henry (*sings*) "Here we go again
                        Moaning low again!!"

Katherine "Yes, Mr Film Producer. No, Mr Film Producer. Three bags full, Mr Film Producer. Mr Film Producer, do tell us about footwear all over again, Mr Film Producer." Kissing his arse.

Henry I suppose you pick up that revolting language from the children.

Katherine I saw the utter contempt—in his cold Slavic eyes. He'll be round for a work session.

Henry No. No, he won't.

Katherine Lying all over the furniture in his stockinged feet. Surrounded by little men from Freeman, Hardy and Willis. Talking through the story line. What's your contribution going to be? The semi-colons? Come to think of it Brunowski probably never heard of a semi-colon.

Henry He's gone.

Katherine What?

Henry And he won't be coming back.

Katherine Or German. Probably a German. They always pretend to come from Austria.

Henry He never mentioned Austria.

Katherine That was his cunning! You were so bloody polite. Collaborating with the Germans . . . That's very typical.

Henry I'm not going to!

Katherine You're not going to what?

Henry I've decided—I shall ring up and say I'm not interested.

Katherine looks at him sympathetically

Katherine (*after a pause*) Poor darling . . . You have that feeling, don't you?

Henry What feeling?

Katherine That he's got away. That you might be missing something—the bus.

Henry It's my life! Standing there full of regrets as the bus draws away into the distance. I remember once. I was at a party.

Katherine When?

Henry Long ago. Before we met.

Katherine (*singing quietly as she starts to clear the table*)
"Long ago and far away
I dreamed a dream one day . . ."

Henry I had an introduction to some people called Bottle. They lived in Enfield. I was told they "swung". I was innocent at the time. Of what "swinging" meant.

Katherine And imagined you'd find the whole family Bottle suspended from the ceiling on trapezes.

Henry Anyway, they invited me to this party. I was standing in the loo when I became aware of many of me. All in similar attitudes. The loo chez Bottle was as rich in mirrors as the Palace of Versailles. When in burst Mrs B.

Katherine Beatrice . . . ?

Henry Bernice Bottle. Gold lamé trousers, stiletto heels, a stretched jersey top. Her front teeth lightly tinted with carmine lipstick.

Katherine I know. She made a proposition. The most boring thing about marriage is having to share your fantasies.

Henry No, it's true! I promise you it's true! "Well," I said, "well, if you really feel like that—urgently."

Katherine Always modest.

Henry "If you feel like that," I said, "let's get the hell out of here and back to my small room in Kilburn High Road."

Katherine That room! Your imaginary heaven.

Henry (*replacing the dining chair*) She was horrified, as if I'd committed some ghastly social blunder. "What?" she said. "Are you suggesting I leave my guests?" As I went out of the door I had the impression she was naked in the dimmed light of the lounge, handing round twiglets. Since then I've felt I've missed some vital experience . . . It was rather like that when Mr Brown left us.

Katherine Do they really do that in Enfield? (*She picks up Sam Brown's hat*)

Henry I believe most Fridays. Except when they're watching Wimbledon.

Katherine He's left his hat.

Henry What?

Katherine (*looking inside it*) Prizunic! M'sieur Brown's left his little tartan hat. (*She puts it down*)

Henry Women don't have fantasies . . .

Katherine Oh, all the time.

Henry What's your fantasy?

Katherine You.

He looks pleased. He pours them both another drink. They drink. He goes to the radiogram

I was coping with some sort of reality. The war. Paul away fighting for his country in army education. I was queueing up for orange juice and dodging doodle bugs. And then I met you. The fantasy began.

Henry New Year's Eve. (*Finding an old record*) The Cathedral Hotel, Guildford.

Katherine A fantasy meal, in time of shortage.

Henry Black Market Communion wine. (*He puts the record on the radiogram*)

Katherine Gin and altars.

Henry Whale steak.

Katherine Moby Dick and chips. (*The record starts to play softly*)

Henry All the men having been called up to study Kafka with your husband . . .

Katherine Eve Tish and her Squadronettes!

They start to dance—a slow foxtrot with lots of Victor Sylvester turns. Katherine sings 'Small Hotel'. The front doorbell rings. They don't hear it

Henry Who wants people?

Katherine (*breaking away from him*) You do! You do, apparently! You want to populate our lives with people! Why do you *tell* me all the time? That's what I don't understand . . . Why *tell* me? (*She turns off the record*)

Henry I haven't told you anything.

Katherine You bring it all back like a little dog—reverently laying corpses, mauled birds, half a rat, on the hearth rug. For Mother to see!

Henry (*singing*) "Here we slide again
Ready to take that ride again . . ."

Katherine Notes on cheque-books! Love letters on the backs of menus! Shirts which you carefully mark with lipstick before you come home at night. For my benefit! Why should I care what weird people you fancy. Just don't bring them all home.

The front doorbell rings again. Intent on quarrelling they do not answer it

Henry I don't fancy him.

Katherine What?

Henry I don't actually fancy Sam Brown.

Katherine (*picking up the notepad by the telephone*) Griselda. *Who is Griselda Griffin?* Tea four-thirty.

Henry Who do you think she is?

Katherine A floosie! A popsie! A little bit of fluff! Tea! How charming. How utterly delightful. Just when I'm reading *Noddy in Toyland* to Henrietta with one hand and prodding groats into Seraphina while she squats on her potty with the other, you'll be giving it to Miss Griselda Griffin in some tousled bed-sitting-room in Oakley Street. And then stagger back for a strong drink and sympathy after a hard day at work. With your pockets full of messages for me to read! (*She throws the pad down*)

Henry (*calmly*) Miss Griselda Griffin is articled to a solicitor of the Supreme Court.

Katherine You're lying!

Henry We shall be meeting in the Kardomah, Fleet Street.

Katherine Why do you have to lie?

Henry Why do you have to pretend?

Katherine Pretend what?

Henry That it's disaster. Fire. War. Pestilence. That you're drowning yourself. That the water is closing over your head.

Katherine Bastard! I am not drowning myself. You're drowning me!

Henry How?

Katherine With your lies. Do you think I mind about Gristle? Of course I don't mind about Gristle. It's the lies I mind, that's all. Why can't you tell the truth for once in your life!

Henry We've chosen the Kardomah so that we can go through forty-two passionate positions under the pastry trolley . . . what do you want?

Katherine What do *you* want?

Henry Freedom. For five minutes. Not to answer questions.

Katherine (*shouting*) Are you? Are you having it off with Gristle? Just say you are. Tell the truth!

Henry (*shouting back*) All right. Yes. I'm having it off with Gristle.

Katherine I hate you!

Henry All right. No! I'm not having it off with Gristle.

Katherine Liar!

Henry (*with very carefully assumed, and maddening, patience and calm*) You could just let me know exactly what it is you want me to say.

Katherine Bloody . . . Barrister!

Katherine picks up the lamp. As she rips it out of the wall there is a flash and darkness as the light fuses. There is a crash in the darkness and then Katherine cries. Katherine and Henry collapse behind the sofa with the lamp, which breaks. There is a great deal of laughter and giggling which changes to sighs and murmurs

The front doorbell rings again and Sam enters, returning to retrieve his hat, and strikes a match

*Somewhere in the gloom Sam sees Henry and Katherine apparently locked
in a death struggle on the floor: he blows out the match, darkness*

You're drowning me!

*After a moment there is the sound of a Hoover. As the Lights come up to
daylight, the whine of the Hoover rises to a crescendo, then dies. When we
can see her, Katherine is alone on the stage, moodily trying to repair the
broken Hoover plug with a knife. The front doorbell rings. Katherine drops
the plug, puts the knife on the table, then opens the door*

    Sam enters

Oh, it's you.

Sam Where's the genius?

Katherine If you mean Henry. He's out. (*She starts to roll the cord of the
Hoover up*)

Sam Oh. Oh, I see. Did he say where . . . ?

Katherine He said—to the Uxbridge Magistrates' Court.

Sam Oh. So that's where he's gone.

Katherine Not necessarily. Where he goes and where he says he goes only
coincide occasionally. (*She pushes the Hoover out into the kitchen as Sam
is speaking*)

Sam He called me. He left a message on my answering service. About our
project, I guess.

Katherine (*coming back from the kitchen*) He's not going to do it. (*She
picks up a doll from under the table, walks a few paces, then throws it back
where it was*)

Sam What?

Katharine (*turning off the electric fire*) He phoned to tell you. He's not
going to do it.

Sam He's not. Any reason in particular?

Katherine We've got too much on our plates.

Sam Pardon me?

Katherine Too many—people. We can't take on you as well. Either of us.
I'm sorry. Look. What's the time? I've got to collect the kids from
nursery and . . .

Sam Look. Mrs Winter—Katherine. (*He moves nearer to her*) Are you
scared of me or something?

Katherine Yes.

Sam What?

Katherine Yes, I'm scared of you, or something.

Sam It's only a script. It's only a little job of work, God dammit. Aren't
you being overly possessive?

Katherine Possessive? Me? Possessive . . . ?

Sam Are you afraid I'm going to take your husband off you?

Katherine (*looking round for an escape*) I've got to get all round John
Barnes' Food Department and . . .

Sam Look, Katherine, are you being exactly fair to Henry?

Katherine (*puzzled*) Fair? I'm married to him, aren't I? What's being fair got to do with it?

Sam I remember. First thing off . . . You suggested to me that he was never out of the kitchen . . . In his apron! Well, our boy seems a fairly normal type of individual . . .

Katherine Our boy! (*Almost laughing in spite of herself*) Our sweet little fellow. Look—if I don't get these kids out of the nursery by three they strap them down on to their pots and read them Bible stories . . .

Sam Katherine! (*He looks at his watch*) It's only midday by now.

Katherine (*desperately, looking hopelessly at the door*) We're standing still . . . The day's going on for ever!

Sam I'd like you to think of me as a human being . . . Forget the film tycoon and all that crap. Ignore the Head of Wardour Screen Promotions and all that bugaboo. Okay, I'm the guy who's in a position to offer your husband remunerative employment. Just think of me as a human person who accidentally got an insight into your private life.

Katherine Accidentally?

Sam That night after dinner, as it so happened, I forgot my hat. Well, your door doesn't seem to shut properly . . .

Katherine We're open to the public.

Sam No-one answered the bell. I thought I'd retrieve it unobtrusively.

Katherine You were here! When . . .

Sam You didn't notice me?

Katherine No—no.

Sam You were busy, I guess.

Katherine (*outraged*) You were spying on us!

Sam (*putting a hand on her shoulder*) Katherine, I am offering you my concern.

Katherine (*moving away from him; angrily*) Not today, thank you!

Sam Not . . . ?

Katherine That's what I have to say to all of you.

Sam All of us?

Katherine All of you who come here offering me offers. I'm stuck here like an Aunt Sally for offers. Once you get your sharp little feet inside the door. Special suction brushes. Cut-price Brillo Pads! Slightly soiled copies of the *Encyclopaedia Britannica*. Gaily coloured books on the subject of Blood, free from Jehovah's Witnesses—and your Concern! Thank you very much. Not today. No, thank you.

Sam You're not happy, are you?

Katherine Oh, for God's sake!

Sam You think you can tell me why?

Katherine Because I can't get anyone to put a new plug on the Hoover. If I got another life it'd be—married to an electrician.

The phone rings. Katherine picks it up. Sam stands watching her. She is tense, gripping the instrument

No. He's not back yet . . . The Magistrates' Court. That's what he said . . . Yes . . . Yes, I'll tell him.

She puts the phone down. Sam looks at her

(*With deep contempt*) Gristle!

Sam (*moving to the door*) Well. You've got the kids to fetch . . .

Katherine (*reluctant now to let him go*) Not till three. Not for hours, actually . . .

Sam I'd better go—and think about another writer . . .

Katherine Don't go. If you don't have to . . .

Sam (*moving back into the room*) I thought I wasn't entirely welcome.

Katherine Oh, you're better than the other things.

Sam Thank you very much! What other things?

Katherine Encyclopaedia men. Jehovah's Witnesses—telephone calls— from Miss Griselda the articled clerk. Why does he have to arrange for her to phone me every hour on the hour? Just in case I might forget her existence . . . ?

Sam Would you like to talk?

Katherine Yes. Yes, I'd like to—I think.

Sam About Henry?

Katherine About anything. It gets so quiet here during the day. Sometimes —sometimes the only way I can hear a bit of intelligent conversation is by switching on the Archers . . .

Sam You know—I'm not really close to Henry. Not intimate. As yet. But from the few times I've met your feller—he struck me—I must say if I'm honest . . .

Katherine How did he strike you?

Sam As amiable. Extremely amiable.

Katherine You know how he struck me? Hard. Did I make a joke? (*She shivers*) How disgusting! It must be infectious. Amiable?

Katherine hears the front door opening and without looking round, raises her voice a little

Oh, certainly. Until he starts throwing the furniture.

Sam Is *that* what happened?

Katherine Didn't you notice? When you were spying on us?

The hall door opens. Henry comes into the room. He is wearing a dark suit and carrying a brief-case

Katherine goes on as if unaware he's arrived

Until he rips the lamps from the wall and uses them—as ammunition!

Henry goes to the table and puts his brief-case down on it

Henry I hear myself say the most incredible things.

Katherine (*moving away and standing by the electric fire and the mantel-piece*) So do I.

Henry In court! I open my mouth and for God's sake Marshall-Hall rides again! There was Bernard in the dock . . .

Sam Hello, Henry. Who . . . ?

Henry Bernard Duffield and I pointed to him—with a finger trembling with emotion . . .

Katherine Such emotional fingers!

Henry "Give him justice", I heard myself say. "The justice he has waited and prayed for all these months. But let it be justice tempered with that mercy which is the hallmark of the Uxbridge and Hillingdon District Magistrates' Court . . ."

Henry laughs. The other two do not

Katherine Was Gristle with you?

Henry What? (*He unpacks some briefs, a typescript, pencils and bills in envelopes, together with children's bricks, from his case*)

Katherine Was the learned Miss Articled Solicitor Griselda in court with you? In your hour of triumph.

Henry Well, as a matter of fact . . . (*He smiles at her*) Yes.

Katherine Then why does she keep ringing me up—to find out where you are?

Henry Oh—well. She had to rush away actually. To an indecent assault in Dagenham . . .

Katherine Tell her to leave me alone, will you?

Henry I suppose she was curious about the result.

Katherine However curious she is. Just tell her to lay off the telephone.

Henry (*remembering with a smile*) "Justice—tempered with that mercy which is the hallmark of the Uxbridge . . ."

Sam Pretty good, that. Did they let him off?

Henry They sent him for trial—at the Old Bailey.

Sam You want to be careful, old friend.

Henry What?

Sam Careful they don't send you for trial. Katherine's been telling me . . .

Henry What . . . ? What's she been telling you?

Sam Only what I saw—with my own eyes.

Katherine He came back after his little tartan hat. The day the Hollywood lamp met an untimely death . . .

Henry Oh. Oh, I see.

Sam And I couldn't help noticing . . .

Henry What?

Sam It appeared to me, chum. Just from the casual glance I took. That you were assaulting your lady wife.

Henry Really?

Sam Striking Katherine.

Henry Is that the impression you got?

Sam I have lived a hell of a lot of life, friend. But I can think of no defence to using physical force against a woman.

Henry Can't you really?

Sam None whatsoever.

Henry Poor Bernard.

Sam Who the hell's Bernard?

Henry Bernard Duffield. My most important client. Come to think of it, by and large my only client. He set out to murder his wife. A huge and ambitious project. Something calling for the full fire-power of the NATO alliance.

Sam And you are defending him.

Henry Brutal Bernard, the Rickmansworth Ripper!

Sam Inhuman.

Henry He bought a long sharp kitchen knife, Sam—and he stole a heavy iron bar from his place of work, and he provided himself with what he describes as a short strangling cord.

Sam Jeasus.

Henry He then went to the *Cricketers* to announce his intentions to at least twenty witnesses, meanwhile absorbing eleven pints of Guinness, nineteen double brandies and twenty-two "Blue Heavens", which turn out to be a mixture of Babycham, port, rum and blackcurrant juice. With his will strengthened, our Bernard set out to commit the crime of the century.

Sam (*hurt*) Henry, baby—I have been sharing you with this criminal.

Henry He climbed up on the roof of the coal bunker and entered the bedroom to deal his wife Maisie instant death . . .

Sam You're not suggesting, I hope, that these Duffields are typical of thousands of perfectly normal married couples all over the world.

Henry Now Maisie had a lover. A Mr Meatyard, the twenty-stone manager of Tescos. Huge and indestructible as herself. And when this vast pair started up in bed Bernard, terrified, fell seventeen feet.

Katherine Poor little fellow.

Henry And so was arrested on his hands and knees, crawling across the allotments with a terrible hangover and two broken ankles. And his victim without a scratch! There is no justice!

Katherine Justice? Is that what you care about?

Henry But we have a defence. A cast-iron defence. They've got the wrong man.

Katherine I know what you're going to say. His wife did it.

Henry Of course. Bernard's innocent! Can't you see? She planned it all.

Katherine Our poor boy. Married to the Boston Strangler!

Henry Mrs Duffield carefully, ruthlessly engineered Bernard's appearance on the roof of the coal bunker, stuffed to the gills with murder weapons and port and Guinness and Babycham and she well knew in her wicked scheming mind that he'd fall and break his fragile little neck.

Pause. Sam looks at Henry, sadly again

Sam Henry—I guess you know I'm feeling sore—sore at you, Henry. Was it a nice way to behave?

Henry To Katherine? We're not going all through that again.

Sam To me! I've been waiting—for a telephone call. Three whole days I waited—for a call. Day and night I waited, feller.

Katherine He's what you might call casual—in human relationships.

Sam And now after keeping me dangling. Katherine says you're about to give me a no-no . . .

Henry Did *she* say that? *She* said it?

Sam What does that mean exactly?

Katherine It probably means he'll do it. It's when he says "yes" you know nothing's going to happen. He said "yes" to putting a new plug on the Hoover.

Henry I didn't say "yes". I said, "Get a man in".

Katherine (*looking at Sam, speaking in a wildly upper class accent*) "Get a man in"—what a perfectly splendid idea! It solves all the problems of married life, doesn't it—getting a man in. Are you going to get a man in to write Sam's script?

Henry No. No, of course not. (*To Sam*) I've been thinking about it. I have really. It's a good idea . . .

Sam Does that mean you'll do it?

Katherine What do you think? Of course it does. Once he'd met you he couldn't bear to let you go.

Sam Well. It was certainly a great evening the three of us had together.

Katherine (*singing to herself*)
"Some enchanted evening
    You will see a stranger . . ."

Sam There was a sort of empathy, I guess. Among the three of us.

Katherine I knew Henry'd cling on to you. For dear life.

Sam I'd be around, Henry. For whenever you'd need me.

Katherine You're something he can't bear to miss. He doesn't want to see you vanish into his fantasies, stark naked and carrying twiglets.

Sam Pardon me. Katherine, I don't know what you're suggesting. But I'm simply interested in your husband as a writer. (*To Henry*) What do you say, old friend? Are we going to work together?

Henry I don't know exactly. (*To Katherine*) Do you want me to?

Katherine (*with sudden outrage*) *Don't ask my permission!*

She is trembling and Sam moves towards her, speaks comfortingly

Sam I want you to feel yourself—included—Katherine.

Katherine In what?

Sam I'm deeply concerned. You shouldn't feel left out. Am I right? Your husband's work causes you loneliness.

Katherine He causes me loneliness. Not his work.

Sam I am concerned about that. I'd like you to know that, Katherine. Deeply concerned . . . I am here. Whenever either of you need me. (*To Henry*) Will you do it?

Henry looks up at Katherine. She looks back at him

Katherine You say, darling. Your need's greater than mine.

Henry All right. We'll start tomorrow.

The Lights fade

Sam exits, taking his hat

Henry brings the typewriter from the sideboard to the table, removes his jacket, and sits. Katherine sits near the fire

The Lights come up to evening, artificial light. Henry starts to build a tower with the children's bricks. Katherine is tense, starts to speak a number of times, stops herself, then finally speaks

Katherine Why can't we talk?
Henry I'm thinking . . .
Katherine What about?
Henry The work. The work in progress. (*He puts another brick on to the tower*)
Katherine Why can't we ever say anything to each other? (*Pause*) Have a conversation . . . ?

Pause. Henry puts on another brick

You don't ever talk, you tell jokes. When do we ever talk—about our lives?
Henry For a living.
Katherine What?
Henry I talk . . . for a living.
Katherine (*stands up, walks about, bored*) Oh, that's your cases. And you tell jokes. When do we ever talk—about our lives?
Henry When I tell jokes. (*The tower falls over, he looks at it ruefully*) All right then. (*He gets up, goes to the sofa, lies down on it*)
Katherine What?
Henry All right. Let's talk.

Pause. Neither of them says anything

Who's going to begin? (*He pulls an imaginary coin out of his pocket*) Toss for service. (*He spins the coin, looks at it*) Toss for service. (*He spins the coin, looks at it*) Heads. You talk first. Toss me a subject. (*Silence*) You're very quiet.
Katherine Yes.
Henry (*pretending to protest*) Why can't we ever have a conversation . . .
Katherine Because you don't ever *mean* anything.
Henry I've got to *mean* what I say? Talking's not enough but I've got to mean it. Now that's a simply impossible demand . . .
Katherine For you.
Henry Forget me.
Katherine Yes.
Henry Just forget me for a moment all together. You say something. With meaning. I'll listen.
Katherine Sam Brown talks. When Mr Brown comes here I hear his voice rising and falling. He seems to be talking to you with some sort of passion.
Henry What am I doing? When Mr Brown's carrying on?
Katherine Agreeing with him!
Henry That's right. In the faint hope he'll shut up. One word of argument and he's good for another three hours.

Pause

Katherine He's rather attractive.

Henry I thought we were supposed to say what we meant.

Katherine I did.

Henry Oh, yes . . .

Katherine I just mean I find Mr Brown rather attractive.

Henry Lovely! If you've got a thing about little tartan hats.

Katherine He's solid. There's something particularly solid about him . . .

Henry Totally solid, I agree. Underneath the hat.

Katherine Don't be so bloody patronizing!

Henry (*frowning*) It's a little bit . . . late. (*He closes his eyes*)

Katherine I want to talk.

Henry All right. Prise my eyelids open with matchsticks. Swing the desk light in my direction . . . (*With a German accent*) "Mr Winter we have ways and ways of making you keep up a conversation . . ."

Katherine Tell me. (*She sits on the sofa, leaning over Henry*)

Henry What?

Katherine What you feel. What you actually *feel*.

His eyes are closed. He does not answer. Silence

Nothing . . .

She moves away from him and sits below the fire. Pause

Henry (*very quietly*) What exactly was the matter with your Aunt Freda?

Katherine becomes tense, does not answer

What did she want to do it for? I've often wondered. I mean, ladies don't just walk into the sea—for no reason at all . . . What was up with her exactly?

Katherine What do you think?

Henry Perhaps she needed a man.

Katherine (*deliberately*) You are disgusting.

Henry (*sleepily*) Am I?

Katherine That's all any woman ever needs, isn't it? Their oats. Their greens. Nookey. Hearthrug pudding.

Henry Is that what you want? I'm a bit sleepy actually.

Katherine She was an old lady. She pressed flowers and she painted in water colours. She lived with two cats in a small cottage near Prestatyn and what upset her was the war. She was frightened of the Germans! She thought they had her on a black list because she was too old for a brothel and too weak for a labour camp and after the invasion she thought they'd take her into Cardiff and put her down! Because she was useless. She would have found absolutely no consolation in hearthrug pudding . . .

Henry If you could wait till the morning. I don't know what it is. I feel distinctly more sprightly in the morning.

Katherine With Henrietta coming into our bed at six o'clock, you're quite safe feeling sprightly in the morning.

Henry (*almost asleep*) Tomorrow—I'll do some work for Sam.
Katherine I never bargained to be married to a writer.
Henry What did you think you'd married?
Katherine As a matter of fact—a gardener.

The Lights fade to a spot on Katherine

As Katherine speaks, Henry takes his jacket and exits up the stairs

You remember—that extraordinary little house. A square house in a field near Guilford. Paul rented it—for what was it during the war? Something? Nothing . . . And—well, we'd only met once before at that dance. New Year's Eve. In the Cathedral Hotel. And, quite unexpectedly I looked out of the window. It was late afternoon. In winter. Quite misty. And I saw him walking up the garden in gumboots.

In the darkness Sam enters and sits on the sofa, a small screwdriver in his hand, putting a new plug on the Hoover

The Lights fade up to bright afternoon

Sam Saw who?
Katherine Henry. Henry, of course.
Sam In what? And he was wearing—what?
Katherine Rubber boots. And an old tweed jacket. With leather patches on the elbows. That's when I decided to marry him.
Sam Rubber boots! That's a great image. Go on . . .
Katherine I thought. We'd live in the country. With oil lamps! The children'd all be sitting round, doing their homework. And I'd hear the soft, slow sound of his gumboots on the gravel. I thought! He'd be standing at the back door—with his hands full of vegetables . . . ! You know what? He never wore those clothes again.
Sam Not the rubbers?
Katherine Or the coat with leather patches. It's my belief he'd hired them. From Moss Bros. Just to come walking up our front garden. How was I to know he'd turn into a man who cooked—and threw lamps at people?
Sam It strikes me, quite honestly . . . you've been misled . . .
Katherine Misled? Totally.
Sam You know, that's a worthwhile theme. For the movie. The woman who has decieved—as to the true identity of her husband.
Katherine By a pair of gumboots!
Sam They're a great image—those rubbers. They've sparked off ideas in me.
Katherine They sparked off ideas in me, too. More's the pity.
Sam How wrong can you be—on the subject of a person! You know how I had you cast the first day I stepped in here . . . ?
Katherine Cast?
Sam As the heavy. The early Bette Davis part. The woman who makes

men feel either fags or impotent. Preferably impotent fags. It was Henry's fault.

Katherine That's what—he led you to believe?

Sam Does she cut ball?—if you will pardon my French. That's what I said to your husband.

Katherine He agreed, of course.

Sam I mean. He didn't bother to argue.

Katherine How very amiable!

Sam He didn't argue.

Katherine If only he would! That's all I want. If only he'd decide something for himself. Of course—he has to think of me like that.

Sam You mean—if he gave you the Debbie Reynolds part he'd have to take a few decisions? (*He finishes the Hoover plug*)

Katherine Debbie Reynolds! I'm not her, am I?

Sam Of course not! You're unique. Very unique. (*He gets up, moves close to her*) Look. Katherine. I'd like to talk to you about this—married couple. It's something I feel we ought to get into. In some kind of depth.

Katherine (*looking at him gratefully*) You want to talk?

Sam The way I see it this isn't going to be just another movie. Any movie. It's something I feel deeply about. Like my own flesh and blood. You know how I see it?

Katherine Tell me.

Sam As two people who got each other wrong, from the beginning.

Katherine Yes!

Sam I feel we should have some further talks. Maybe just the two of us.

Katherine You want—conversation?

Sam Could we maybe—go to dinner?

Katherine (*doubtful*) Dinner?

Sam Just the two of us one night . . .

Katherine (*nervously*) Not dinner. I don't think so . . . (*Looking at the Hoover*) You've done it?

Katherine takes the plug as if it were something very precious, and plugs it in. The Hoover lights up and roars. She looks at him with deep gratitude, then unplugs it. They are looking at each other all the time. The telephone rings, breaking into the moment. She answers it

Excuse me? The Westminster . . . Oh, Mr MacFeeling . . . No. It's all right . . . Yes. You can speak to my husband.

She suddenly hands the phone to Sam, who takes it, surprised

Katherine quickly pushes the Hoover out of the room to L of the stairs

Sam (*into the phone, helplessly*) Hullo? . . . No. I'm sorry. No—I'm just someone who happened—to be here.

Sam replaces the receiver and exits through the front door, looking upstairs as he goes

The Lights fade

*Henry enters and sits at the table, picks up a script and starts to read it.
Sam enters with a similar script, reading*

*The Lights come up to evening, with artificial lighting on. Henry gets up
nervously, and looks over his shoulder anxiously to see Sam's reaction. There
is none. Sam puts the pages carefully on the table*

You want to talk a little?

Henry Not really.

Sam I mean, audiences today weren't born yesterday, old chum. They're
going to be two jumps ahead.

Henry What of?

Sam Of you! "This is another one", they will say, "about two people who
are married." It'll empty the Odeon, Leicester Square quicker than
"God Save The Queen".

Henry But they are.

Sam What?

Henry Married.

Sam Look, this is just spit balling—just off the top of the milk. Suppose
they're *not* married. Suppose they're shacked up. Interesting? More of
today?

Henry I thought we wanted to investigate what keeps a marriage going.

Sam All right. You tell me. What does?

Henry (*after a pause*) Fear.

Sam Fear? Fear of what exactly?

Henry If they knew that . . .

Sam Well?

Henry They'd probably leave each other. Are you drinking today?

Sam Just coffee. Let's just think about the big box-office grossers. Can't
we work a brutal car chase in here somewhere?

Henry (*looking round the room*) I should think so. We've had almost
everything else. I'll make you some coffee.

Henry exits to the kitchen

*There is a pause, then Sam jumps up excitedly and goes to shout to Henry
through the kitchen door*

Sam What about this, Henry? I think I'm on to something! Oh, Christ!
I am *very* excited. It's a funny bugger, isn't it?

Henry (*off*) What?

Sam Inspiration! Suppose they're . . . Listen to this carefully, baby.
Suppose *our* baby are—our married people. We make them—a couple
of fellers!

Henry comes back from the kitchen

Henry I'm afraid coffee's out of the question.

Sam What?

Henry Another part of the house has given up the struggle.

Sam Forget it. My idea! What's your reaction?

Henry A couple of fellers? That's exactly what they are.

Sam (*looking at him with sad disapproval*) Henry. I think I know you well enough now to say this. Do you treat marriage with sufficient respect?

Katherine comes down the stairs into the room. She has changed, looking very smart, carrying a handbag, ready to go out. She pauses a moment to look at her face in the mirror over the fireplace

I'm not asking you for gimmicks, Henry. Okay, forget two queens shacked up which could be interesting. Forget the action sequences. Forget the box-office even. Try and imagine two people mistaken about each other from the start.

Katherine goes and finds a new packet of cigarettes hidden away among the books

Does that thought surprise you?

Henry (*looking at Katherine*) My couple—understand each other only too well.

Sam Henry—I can tell by these thirty pages. You need help with this one. Two heads is what you need, Henry. My friend, I think you'll like what I'm going to suggest.

Henry What're you going to suggest?

Katherine goes and sits in a central position—takes a case out of her handbag and carefully fills it with the cigarettes. The two men are on each side of her, looking at her as they discuss her

Sam A collaboration? With your wife?

Henry (*after a pause; looking at Sam, amazed*) You want Katherine? To write your movie?

Sam To help you. I figure it's a pretty good team.

Henry Have you asked her—by any chance?

Sam Not yet. Do you think I'll get a "No. No"?

Henry Samuel. If you were shooting a TV Commerical . . .

Sam I have done so. The greatest . . .

Henry And if you approached the Vatican and asked the Pope to raise his arms over Saint Peter's Square at Easter and give a short plug for fully fashioned Gossamer Durex . . . Do you think you'd get a "No. No"?

Sam You mean the actual Pope? Live?

Henry You want my wife live, don't you? Dead or alive?

Sam Do you have anything—against this project, Katherine?

Henry (*coming in before Katherine can answer*) It's not a project to her. It's the beginning of the end. It's the Black Death. The dry rot in the basement. The start of group sex in the children's playroom and Mes-

calin in the Ostermilk. She fears it. She detests it. It makes her blood
run cold . . .

Katherine So why do you do it?

Henry You really want to know?

Sam Your motivation, old chum.

Henry Money. (*He goes over to the table, tosses up a pile of bills like autumn
leaves*)
Rates. Light! Gas! This small corner of Belsize Park is about to opt out
of the Industrial Revolution.

Katherine There's always enough—for a bloody Hollywood table lamp.

Henry (*to Sam*) You've heard of places where old people go to die? This
is where they go to be born. All those millions of spermatozoa—which
usually float off into innocent waste—say, "Look, this is seventy-nine
Alexandra Drive. Cling on, darling. They buy bikky pegs here by the
shipload". This isn't a home, Sam. It's a reservoir for an expanding
population. (*He goes to the table, picks up the script, looks at it sadly*)
Is there a bit of it you like?

Sam You want me to be brutally frank?

Henry I'd rather have a little dishonest praise.

Sam (*putting a hand on Henry's shoulder*) Why don't we wait, until I get
Katherine's reaction?

Katherine stands up. They both look at her, expectant

Katherine I think it's disgusting!

Henry You haven't read it . . .

Katherine This is Sam's project. It's like his child. He's nursed it. Cared
about it. Deeply. And you stand there and tell him your only interest
in his story of married life is paying the gas bill. It's sordid! That's what
you are—mercenary!

Henry (*outraged*) *Me?* And who's always on—day in, day out about
MacFeeling at the Westminster?

Katherine Mr MacFeeling's been spoken to—which is more than you'd
ever do. (*She moves to the front door*) Shall we go now, Sam?

Sam moves with her

Henry What's happening?

Katherine Sam's taking me to dinner.

Henry We'll have to get a baby sitter.

Katherine We've got one.

Henry Who?

Katherine You. There's nothing much except Seraphina's ten o'clock feed.

Henry Well, about that. It might be difficult . . .

Katherine Why not ask Gristle to help? Or don't articled ladies qualify
in changing nappies? (*Almost hopeful*) Don't you want me to go—are
you going to argue?

Henry No. Of course you can go. I'll be all right.

Katherine and Sam move towards the door

Where are you going, actually?

Katherine Trattoria Alfresco. The one you thought looked nice. By the tube station.

Henry Enjoy yourselves.

Sam and Katherine exit

(*As the front door shuts on them*) Good-bye. Feller.

They have gone. He rushes to the telephone, dials a number, speaks in an absurd Army officer's voice

Hullo. North Thames Gas Board, Emergency Service? . . . This is an emergency. My name's Winter. Henry Winter. Seventy-nine, Alexandra Drive, and I've been overseas. Central Africa, actually. Government service. I returned to find my gas cut off . . . Well, I never got my gas bill. How would I get a gas bill in Central Africa? There's an almighty cheque—in the post. Tomorrow morning you'll be astonished and delighted and be able to open a new gas works, most probably . . . Look, I've got starving children here. I'm desperate . . . Well, yes. I suppose so. Yes. A person can still be desperate, even if he's got an electric kettle.

He puts down the phone. It rings

(*Answering it*) Oh, it's you. It's you. Miss Griffin, darling . . . Bernard? . . . Bernard Duffield . . . Yes . . . Yes, of course we need the doctor . . . To say that Bernard was incapable of forming the intention of blowing his nose. That he had no idea of right and wrong. That he couldn't tell the difference between a kiss on the mouth and a bash over the head with an iron bar. Just like the rest of us. Yes, I am a bit peculiar tonight. My wife's gone off. With a fat, old film producer from Yeovil. Well, not all that fat actually, or old . . . See you? Of course I want to see you . . . At the Kardomah . . . We've got a date, haven't we? Miss Griffin . . . Where have you gone, Miss Griffin? (*He listens to the cut-off phone*) Vanished. (*He puts down the phone. Then, bored, dials a longer, country number*) Hullo . . . Hullo, Mum . . . Well, I've been busy. Rather busy . . . No, I haven't been irritating Katherine . . . Yes. I have been treating her well. I'm writing a film . . . A film . . . Well, a film *is* photographs, Mother . . . Yes. But you have to write words for the people to say . . . Yes . . . Yes, it is rather killing, actually. No, Mother, it is not an opera singer . . . Yes, I know you saw Grace Moore in *Love Me Tonight* . . . No, I don't suppose it will be as good as that. This one about *us*. Me and Katherine . . . Why are you laughing, Mother? You think that's a funny idea? I hope it turns out funny. Well, not as funny as that. Look, what I was ringing you up about. You can't think of any sort of simple dinner you can cook in an electric kettle . . . Please . . . Please stop *laughing*, Mother!

He puts down the telephone. Bored, he goes to the waste-paper basket, takes

*out the wine bottle, puts it to his eye and gets the last drop in it, drops it
back into the waste-paper basket. He goes out into the kitchen and returns
immediately with the plastic bath which now contains a baby's bottle,
nappies, an alarm clock, an electric kettle, a tin of Ostermilk, measuring jug
and ladle. He winds up the clock and puts it on the mantelpiece. Looks up
at the book shelves and thinks of something. Climbs on a chair, finds an old
black address book carefully concealed behind the books on the top shelf
and dials a number with excitement*

(*On the phone*) Stella, Stella, that's exactly what I like . . . Well, is it
seven years, is it, really? Well, a few children. Well, about twenty . . .
No, what I like is, what I really appreciate, Stella, is that you're *there*!
When I ring. Waiting! No nonsense about it. Well now, Stella. What
are you doing? . . . Cooking a chicken. It's nearly cooked. Well, why
don't you wrap it all up in that silver paper stuff and bring it round . . .
Yes. I'm alone. To all intents and purposes, totally alone. In the world
. . . Oh, you're cooking it for Brownjohn. Oh, *Brownjohn*. Who's he? . . .
You married him. Not the man who used to leap out and hit the car
with an umbrella every night when we turned into your road? . . . Am
I desperate? Of course I'm not desperate. As a matter of fact, it's pretty
eventful—life in Belsize Park.

The alarm clock goes off

I have to rush now. People coming. Ring me again some time. (*He puts
down the phone and hurries to turn off the clock. Then he plugs in the electric
kettle. He has the address book in his mouth as he starts to make up the
food. He sits at the table with the chart beside him and ladles out about
eight measures, getting it all over his trousers and the table. He puts back
one scoopful, puts the lid on the tin, brushes the powder off his trousers,
then brushes it from the table on to his trousers again. He gives up in
despair, takes the book out of his mouth, glances in it, gives a little whistle
of surprise and, on an impulse, dials a number*) Is Mr Bottle there, please?
. . . Oh . . . Edwin Bottle that end? This is Henry . . . Don't you remember? Henry Winter . . . Yes . . . Yes, indeed. Very long time no see.
Look, what I wanted to ask you was—you're not having a party tonight
by any chance? . . . Oh well, I just thought you might . . . How's Bernice?
. . . (*Incredulously*) She's *what*? (*Hushed and solemn*) I'm sorry . . . No,
I hadn't heard. I'm really sorry. (*He puts down the phone*) Bernice.
Dead . . .

*The kettle starts to give a low whistle. He is about to pick it up when the
doorbell rings. He switches off the kettle and goes to answer the door*

*Griselda Griffin enters, carrying a brown paper carrier bag and a brief-
case. She is young, enthusiastic, a solicitor's articled clerk, pretty, with a
rather breathless, upper-class accent.*

Griselda You're really alone?
Henry Alone. Yes. Totally. Of course. (*He quickly switches off the main*

lights and turns on the electric fire, producing a romantic glow) Are you
going to stay a little while?

Griselda I can't believe it. (*She puts the paper bag on the table, looking
round*)

Henry No, I can't, either.

Griselda (*afraid*) She really isn't here.

Henry As you see.

Griselda I'm afraid of your wife.

Henry I know you are. (*He takes her brief-case and puts it down by the
sofa, then helps her off with her coat and puts it over the back of the chair*)
We all are. I'm afraid of my wife. Come to think of it, my wife's scared
to death of my wife. Why don't you sit down?

Griselda No reason. (*She sits suddenly on the sofa in front of the electric
fire, warms her hands, shivering*) I rang the doctor for Bernard.

Henry For Bernard? Well, we've got to look after Bernard, haven't we?
I worry about him naturally, most of the time. (*He sits beside her on the
sofa then slides, romantically, down on to the floor*)

Griselda Why? He's not your only case, is he?

Henry (*on the defensive*) My only case? Of course not. I've got others . . .
I've got cases—some other cases . . .

*There is the sound of a door banging upstairs and a number of children
shouting*

Griselda (*frightened*) What was that?

Henry Mice.

Griselda I wouldn't've come. If you hadn't said you were alone.

Henry No. No, of course not . . . (*He takes her hand*) Well now, about
Bernard.

Griselda Mr Fidella thinks he ought to plead guilty.

Henry Nonsense. We've got a defence. No men's rea . . .

Griselda What?

Henry His mind—was on something else at the time.

Griselda On what?

Henry Who knows?

Griselda Mr Fidella said that Bernard Duffield must be taken to have
intended the natural and probable consequences of his act.

Henry Oh, yes?

Griselda The natural and probable consequences. That's what he says.

Henry (*gently stroking Miss Griffin as he talks*) So when Bernard courted
Maisie, when he placed a hand on those huge knickers in the quiet
back row of the Essoldo, he no doubt intended it should all end up in
a short strangling cord and him with a pair of broken ankles crawling
across the allotments . . . I mean any fool could see that coming a mile
off. Is that what Mr Fidella says?

Griselda Well . . .

Henry Come to think of it it's something I've never done.

Griselda What?

Henry Intended the natural and probable consequences of my acts.

Griselda You never told her, did you?

Henry What?

Griselda You never told your wife. Not about me.

Henry Of course not.

Griselda What would've happened. If you had?

Henry (*casually*) Oh, I suppose . . . Bloodshed.

Griselda What?

Henry Armageddon! An explosion which would have rocked the very foundations of Belsize Park. The casualties would have been enormous.

Griselda (*looks at him*) Are you lying? I think you tell her everything. Bring everything home to Mum. (*She gets up and looks in the mirror*)

Henry You are all alike! It's extraordinary. Wherever one looks there is another one of you standing there. (*He rises and looks at her thoughtfully*)

Griselda I couldn't have put up with it, if you'd told her. Of course, I wouldn't mind now.

Henry Now?

Griselda Now she's gone.

Henry Gone?

Griselda Hasn't she? With a film producer?

Henry Yes. Yes, of course. Sit down. Don't look so gloomy, Miss Griffin. From now on life's going to be simple. Calm—simple. We shall sit in the Kardomah and not care who knows it . . . (*He puts his hand on her shoulders*)

Griselda And go out in the evenings?

They sit on the sofa

Henry And go out in the evenings, most probably . . . And there will be no feelings of impending disaster. Why is it that I seem to have filled all the women I've met with feelings of impending doom? I'm cheerful, basically. Naturally cheerful. Oh, yes, and we'll get Bernard off. The future, Miss Griffin, is incredibly bright. (*He starts to stroke her gently*)

Griselda (*looking up at him admiringly*) Tell me . . .

Henry Yes, Miss Griffin.

Griselda How are we going to get Bernard off?

Henry He was filled to the eyes with "Blue Heavens" for a start.

Griselda "A man cannot wilfully deprive himself of an intention . . ." R. *v.* Snoddin.

Henry Try not to get to know any law, Miss Griffin. You'll find it a great disadvantage in the legal profession.

Griselda "If he does so he must be presumed to have that intention which he would have had had he not been incapable of such intention."

Henry Let's not get too subtle, Miss Griffin. A criminal act requires a criminal intention. (*He strokes her on the thigh*)

Griselda But not an intention to do the precise act charged. For example. If I climb down a chimney with the intention of raping the cook . . .

Henry What things you get up to—at Law Society evening classes!

Griselda And it happens to be the cook's night off. (*Triumphantly*) I have still entered—with felonous intent . . . "Although the actus be frustrated."

Henry You little devil! Who said that?

Griselda Lord Bogden of Midhurst. R. *v*. Blenkinhall.

Henry Fuck Lord Bogden of Midhurst.

He is about to kiss her—she breaks away, goes to her carrier bag

Griselda I brought this . . . (*She takes a short orange nylon baby doll nightdress out of the carrier bag and holds it up in front of her*)

Henry Why?

Griselda You've never seen it before. When you said you were all alone— I thought. Now I can at least wear a nightie.

Griselda turns and, carrying the nightie, goes quickly upstairs

Henry No . . . No, please . . . (*He goes quickly to the telephone, dials three figures*) Enquiries? I want an alarm call, please. Would you wake me up—(*he looks at his watch*)—in thirty seconds time . . . Just a cat nap actually.

Miss Griffin is back, in panic, carrying her nightdress

Griselda There's a child, standing on the stairs. (*She stuffs the nightdress back into the bag*)

Henry Look. Miss Griffin . . .

Griselda Looking at me with accusing eyes. Is it one of yours?

Henry Do you want me to check?

The telephone rings

(*Answering it*) My alarm what? . . . (*He remembers, and speaks as if to Katherine*) Oh, hullo, darling . . . Tonight? No—well, yes, darling . . . Yes, I suppose so . . . No . . . The children . . . Yes—yes, of course I understand . . . All right. (*He replaces the receiver and looks sadly at Miss Griffin*) She's coming back!

Griselda When?

Henry Now.

Griselda (*replacing the nightdress in her case*) But her film producer . . .

Henry Apparently—let her down . . .

Griselda (*picking up her bag*) Oh, God, will it tell her?

Henry tries to get her into her coat, but keeps missing the armhole. Finally he puts the coat under one of her arms and the bag under another and pushes her up to the door, all during the following speeches

Henry What?

Griselda That child! That child'll tell her I was here, and there'll be—what did you say? Total war?

Henry Don't worry, Miss Griffin. The children are completely uninterested in our activities. All the same—you'd better go.

Miss Griffin goes

Henry gets the bottle and Ostermilk tin out of the plastic bath and goes on with his preparations

The front door opens. Miss Griffin is back. She grabs her paper bag

Griselda I left this. (*She looks at him*) You didn't want her to find it, did you?
Henry No. No, of course not. But if she did—and if war broke out—would I intend the natural and probable consequences of my acts? Can you tell me that, Miss Griffin—from a legal point of view?
Griselda I'm frightened.
Henry I'm—I'm sorry.

A taxi is heard stopping in the street outside

Go on—run for safety, Miss Griffin. Out through the garden. They're coming over now. Things are hotting up. Take cover.

Henry grabs Miss Griffin and pushes her through the kitchen door, hearing the taxi door slam as he returns

Henry rushes to the main lights and switches them on, then picks up the kettle

Katherine and Sam enter through the front door

Did you have a good time?

Katherine takes the kettle

Katherine I'll do Seraphina's food. (*She pours water into the bottle*)

There is an awkward pause

Sam How are you, feller . . . ?
Henry Quite well, thank you. (*He goes to the radiogram, looks among the records for something to play*) Nice dinner, Katherine?
Katherine I didn't notice.
Henry Well, Did you get a "no-no"?
Sam Katherine has agreed—to come into the project. She has a whole lot to offer—in the way of perception and genuine understanding.
Henry Corruption!
Sam What?
Henry Didn't she tell you, she'd get corrupted?
Katherine I might get rescued.

Henry looks at her, says nothing

Sam Of course we'll be glad to have your help, Henry. On a purely working basis. Katherine agrees. You still have something to offer.

Henry Big of her.

Sam I told her . . . You might find it too painful.

Henry What?

Sam Working along with Katherine and me. Might be just too painful for you. Under the circumstances. It's sure going to be a tough one for you, feller.

Henry It's only a film, isn't it? I mean. (*Looking at records*) For God's sake. It's only a story.

Katherine Not exactly. (*She puts the teat on the bottle and shakes it*)

Henry What do you mean?

Katherine Oh, it's not just tonight. You know it's been going on ever since we met.

Henry Going on? What's been going on exactly?

Katherine Battles . . . Lies . . . Plotting and scheming! I'm tired. I'm tired out. I want peace, that's all. I want to wake up in the morning and know it's not going to be a war . . .

Henry Why don't you say it?

Katherine All right. I'm going to marry Sam.

Sam Naturally, old friend, we wanted you to be the first to know.

Henry puts on the record. Buddy Holly starts to sing

Record "Do you remember, baby
　　　　　　Last September, baby
　　　　　　How you held me tight——

Henry sits on the sofa

　　　　　　—Each and every night?
　　　　　　Well—WOOPS A DAISY
　　　　　　How you drove me crazy
　　　　　　But I guess it doesn't matter any more."

Henry (*quietly*) Be my guest.

The song continues, as—

the CURTAIN *slowly falls*

ACT II

The same

Before and as the CURTAIN *rises, the record is playing. Katherine, Sam and Henry are in exactly the same position as at the close of Act I*

Record "You go your way and I'll go mi-i-ine
Now and for ever till the end of time.
Golly gee! What have you done to me?
But I guess it doesn't matter any more.
There's no use in me a cry-y-y-ing
I've done everything 'n now I'm sick of trying.
I've lost all my nights
'N wasted all my days
Over YOU-OU-OU . . ."

Katherine goes to the radiogram and switches it off

Katherine Don't you think we ought to talk?

Henry Thrash it around a bit? I expect you'd enjoy that.

Katherine Just for once in your life—couldn't we have a serious discussion?

Henry Oh. Is *that* why you're doing it?

Katherine What?

Henry So we can have a serious topic for discussion. I mean, isn't that going rather far? Couldn't we just think up a few good debating subjects?

Katherine (*to Sam*) It's hopeless. He'll never talk.

Henry Talk? Of course I'll talk. I'll talk for hours. It's my one talent. "This House Believes that Sex Without Marriage is like an Egg Without Salt." I will now call upon Mr Samuel Brown of Keble College to propose the motion.

Katherine (*to Sam*) He won't say anything . . .

Henry What is there to say? I suppose you've given this matter some thought?

Sam Thought? It's more of a gut reaction. Where I come from people are accustomed to think with their guts.

Henry How peculiar. I suppose they digest in their skulls and their mouths, as you would so elegantly say, are full of shit.

Katherine That wasn't funny. That was disgusting and not very funny.

Henry Where was it then? This land of gastronomic cerebration?

Sam Poland.

Katherine Sam grew up in New York. The West Side . . .

Henry Universal man?

Sam All right, Hank. Where were you raised?

Henry The rough end of Godalming. Want to make something of it?

Katherine (*sighing*) Very funny.

Henry I don't see why there's anything necessarily funny about Godalming.

Katherine For six long years I've been looking for a man without a sense of humour.

Henry Well, you've certainly found one.

Katherine He means what he says. It isn't a joke, thank God.

Henry Oh, he means it. That doesn't mean it isn't a joke.

Katherine Jokes! I hate jokes. I've been drowning in jokes, sinking in them. Smothered by them! When our children fall over they don't cry. they make jokes which is what he taught them.

Henry (*to Sam*) She'd rather they cried.

Katherine Oh, yes. Yes, much rather. You don't know how I look round this family and long for tears. Tears would be like rain in a desert of puns.

Henry You and old Sam Brown have learnt to cry together?

Katherine I honestly think he's serious.

Henry (*rising*) Are you, Sam? Are you serious? (*He inspects Sam closely*) Yes. He's serious. (*To Katherine*) Do you fancy him, quite honestly?

Katherine I feel—seriously involved.

Henry (*sitting again*) Oh, really, and when did you get hooked? Has old Sam been dropping in then, most afternoons when I'm down in the Temple? Has he helped you pick up the kids from playgroup in the back of the old Apha? How did you do your courting? Across a crowded bathroom, launching plastic ducks and towelling down my daughters in front of the electric fire? "Don't interrupt, Henrietta—Mummy's getting a proposal of marriage." You make my blood cold.

Katherine Doesn't it remind you of something?

Henry What?

Katherine You used to come round in the afternoons—when I was married to Paul. You used to sit on the edge of the bath, but you made jokes . . .

Henry I'm sorry. I should have made sounds of serious concern.

Sam I am seriously concerned—about your wife, Hal.

Henry Concerned! And I suppose your concern's better than my concern. Yours is real genuine, loving Hi Fi, Three D, fully stereo, gorgeous Panavision concern and mine's only small time mini concern from Godalming. Why should we have finer feelings—just because he never makes a joke?

Katherine Sam was concerned by that appalling incident . . .

Henry What incident?

Sam That was a pretty lethal lamp you threw at her, feller.

Henry (*incredulously*) I threw? *I?* (*To Katherine*) You believe that, don't you . . . ?

Sam You could have done Kate a permanent injury.

Katherine He's proud of that. "Put poppies round that crack in the plaster", he said, "and blow the last post there on Armistice Day."

Henry Did I? Did I say that . . . ?
Katherine He loves to get sentimental about our old battles.
Sam Look, Henry. We've talked about this, Kate and I. Over and over. And we can't see any other way out.
Henry It's bigger than both of you.
Katherine Shut up!
Sam It's a pretty sizeable thing. Yes. Of course, you'll fight like hell to keep her. I respect that.
Henry Do you?
Sam Sure. Been a fighter all my life. A Polack kid—raised in a country where every man and boy was competing for his territory . . .

Henry begins to hum Western film music—the tune from "The Big Country"

We *had* to fight.
Henry From Wyoming to Montana. From Devil's Gulch to the Old Red River——
Katherine Shut up!
Henry —I look around and I'm mighty proud to tell you, boy, it's Sam Brown's country!
Katherine Stop it . . .
Sam You'll fight me over this, naturally.
Katherine Are you sure he will? (*She turns her back on them and the audience*)
Henry Or is it hopeless? Am I a loser, eh, Sam? Samuel. May I call you Mr Brown? What're you offering my wife? Concern? Deep—deep emotions—like money?
Sam I certainly hope to bring Katherine happiness.
Henry Happiness? Dear Mr Brown. That's your first boob, if I may say so. Bring my wife happiness and she won't even bother to unwrap the parcel. She doesn't want happiness. She wants tragedy. She wants war! Every morning when she gets up she goes over the top, with incredible courage and her teeth gritted to breakfast. She doesn't want perfume. She wants the smell of gunpowder. Death and destruction. With explosive electric light fittings flying through the air. She won't walk beside you down an English lane, old chum . . . but all the long way into the sea at Prestatyn. Leave your clothes here, brother. With a little note for your relatives.

Katherine runs into the kitchen and bangs the door. Sam goes quickly into the kitchen after her

Sam (*calling from the kitchen*) Look out! She's turning on the gas taps . . . She's got the oven open. She's turning on the gas.
Henry Let her.

There is the sound of a struggle from the kitchen

Sam (*off*) Kate! Come away from them! Now leave it, honey. Life's good, darling. Life's going to be very good to us from now on. Sam's got you now. Sam's going to take good care of you . . . *Leave those gas taps alone!*

Henry Let her turn them on . . .

Sam appears at the kitchen door

Sam Did you say, "Let her turn them on"?

Henry Why not? They've cut off the gas.

Sam You *bastard*!

Katherine comes out of the kitchen, walks past Sam

Katherine I went to make coffee, that's all.

Sam Is that right?

Henry She went to make some coffee, that's all.

Sam In the oven? Do you make coffee in the oven?

Katherine I was looking for the gas.

Henry They've removed it. You see, I haven't paid the bill.

Katherine (*to Sam*) You grabbed hold of me. I don't know why you grabbed hold of me. I just thought it was time . . . we all had some coffee.

Sam You haven't paid the bill . . .

Henry It's been waiting here. For you.

Sam What?

Henry I understand you are about to take over this leaking enterprise? (*To Sam*) It's all yours. They're upstairs. Waiting for you. All those hungry little mouths. So you want an inventory? Three bright red cast-iron saucepans her mother gave us, a broken iron and an early English washing machine. (*He picks up bills and starts to stuff them into Sam's pockets*) Here . . . ! Here . . . ! The horrible results of unforeseen quarter days. Look—brown envelopes—fresh and untouched. You can read them together—in the long winter evenings by the dying plastic coal of her ex-husband's electric fire. Samuel Brown. This is My Life! Take it . . .

Sam looks at Katherine. She is looking back at him, smiling

Go on. I meant it. Be my guest.

Sam stands looking from one to the other, hesitating

Sam Well now. Wait a minute.

Henry What's the matter, Boy? Feeling nervous? Stand straight now. You'll make a wonderful target for table lamps. I wish I could stay here all night. To listen to you two saying meaningful things to each other. But I must go now. There are people waiting for me. I know you'll both be very, very happy. (*He does not move*)

Sam (*looking from one to the other, confused, uncertain*) I—I—I—I can't do it to you, Henry.

Sam turns quickly and exits. The front door slams after him

Henry and Katherine are left alone. A child calls from upstairs

Katherine exits upstairs to answer the child

Henry, all alone, switches on the radio. It is playing the "Appassionata" sonata of Beethoven. He lets it play, then goes and sits on the sofa. He is smiling as the Lights fade to Black-Out

When the Lights come up again as before, Henry has gone, the music has stopped, and Katherine is sitting crouched in front of the electric fire. She is shivering slightly

Henry comes in from the stairs with a tray of children's supper

Henry Seraphina's settled. I've settled Seraphina. (*He goes into the kitchen, speaking off*) Seraphina's settled. She actually used her pot. I promised her a bit of chocolate. As a reward. Probably have the most disastrous effect on her future life. At dinner-parties. (*He comes back into the room*) I mean, every time anyone offers her an "After Eight" she'll dash off to the loo.

Katherine (*after a pause, seeming a long way off, in a trance*) What did you say . . . ?

Henry Every time anyone offers her an "After Eight" . . . Don't bother. (*He goes to the table, finds a brief tied in pink tape*) Court tomorrow. (*He moves to a chair, sits, pulls the tape off the brief and starts to read it*) What're you going to do tomorrow? (*Pause; Katherine does not answer*) You going to do something nice tomorrow?

Katherine (*after a long pause*) Approach death. By inches.

Pause

Henry (*who has not listened*) That'll be nice . . .

Katherine (*suddenly sinking her face in her hands*) Oh my God!

Henry (*not looking up*) What did you say?

Katherine (*lifting her desperate face*) Nothing. Absolutely nothing.

Henry (*not looking at her*) Sorry, I thought you said something. (*He takes out a pencil, starts to mark the brief*) It makes a change, doesn't it? I'm in court making money. Well—somehow we must make money. Now Sam's left us—and his profitable assignment. I was relying on Sam for the new kitchen lino.

Katherine (*looking at him in amazed desperation*) It's incredible!

Henry (*not looking at her, reading his brief*) Italian ceramic tile lino. Make the bathroom look like the baths of Caracala.

Katherine You are incredible!

Henry (*working*) With the original Ancient Roman Ascot heater. We might have had central heating. Without Sam, I suppose—we've got to soldier on with the old Ascot . . .

Katherine (*getting up and starting to walk about nervously*) Talk about something else . . .

Henry What?

Katherine Will you please talk about something else?

Henry (*after a pause*) All right, what? (*Pause*) What would you like me to talk about? (*Pause*) The weather? The kids? Myself? My case? (*He puts down the brief, looks at Katherine*) I'll tell you about my case. Would that pass the time? I mean we can't go to bed yet, can we? It'd be ridiculous—to settle down for the night before Daniel—shall I tell you?

Katherine If you like.

Henry It's an attempted murder.

Katherine (*positively, agreeing*) Yes!

Henry A husband who tried to murder his wife. I'm defending him.

Katherine Of course!

Henry Why?

Katherine It's bloody appropriate!

Henry His name is Bernard Duffield.

Katherine His name is *you*!

Henry (*looking at her, surprised*) What?

Katherine (*almost shouting*) Be my guest! (*She sits as before*)

Henry Oh, come on . . .

Katherine You don't want me, do you? You don't want me in the least. Why am I walking slowly? I should run—I should run into the water. Shall I give you that? Shall I? Freedom. Freedom for little nights in Enfield and little afternoons with Gristle and have her round here after you've put Serena on her pot and told Daniel about your heroic feats in the Hendon Magistrates' Court. You wanted to get rid of me!

Henry You really minded!

Katherine What?

Henry You minded when I said that. "Be my guest."

Katherine Minded! (*She sits in the chair*) Of course I minded.

Henry So you ran into the kitchen.

Katherine To make coffee!

Henry In the oven?

Katherine I went to make the coffee.

Henry And Sam Brown became very embarrassed and bolted. In disarray. I do miss his whiskey—I'm sorry. (*Rising*) If I said the wrong thing . . .

Katherine (*outraged*) If!

Henry (*soothing*) But it worked! It made Mr Brown run a mile. It was . . . remarkably successful?

Katherine You're not saying that's why you did it?

Henry Of course. I was fighting for you. (*He squats on the floor beside her*)

Katherine Fighting? You were lying down.

Henry That's how the Indians fought the British Raj. that's how Gandhi fought. He lay down in his little loin cloth and the brutal Ghurkas were too ashamed to march over him and break his glasses.

Katherine Oh, I'm sorry. I didn't recognize you. (*She gets up, disgusted*) Anyone less than Gandhi . . .

Henry The Mahatma was a very sexy person. When young. I am a bit like him. Yes. You see it worked!

Katherine I don't believe you! You're lying again. Always lying. (*She sits by the table*)

Henry People like Sam are very suggestible.

Katherine You're not going to pretend that you were pretending?

Henry (*rising, pleased with his ingenuity*) You know old Sam. He can't read a book unless it's *Book of the Month*. He can't go to the movies unless there are queues around the block and it's impossible to get in. He won't even have a disease unless it's been sanctified by an article in the *Reader's Digest*. I saw at once. The only way to get rid of him was to pretend you were not exactly the hot little property he'd bargained for. He was expecting to pay the earth for you. He just couldn't put up with the discovery that you were being given away like a Green Shield Stamp.

Katherine You are disgusting!

Henry What did you expect me to do? Challenge him to a duel?

Katherine Yes. Yes, I'd've liked that . . .

Henry (*kneeling beside her suddenly, his arm round her*) Don't be ridiculous! I had to use some sort of guile. Well, all I'm pointing out to you, darling, is—it worked. It worked superlatively!

She smiles faintly

You may laugh—but there's something to be said for a good basic training before the Hendon magistrates . . .

Katherine (*almost laughing*) He did look tremendously confused.

Henry I thought so.

Katherine He left quickly.

Henry That's the one disadvantage of a nice fixed universe like Sam's. It's tremendously easy to turn upside down.

Katherine (*looking at him, uncertainly*) You wanted to get rid of him?

Henry Of course.

Katherine Really? Really and truly?

Henry Really and truly.

Katherine Very, very clever . . .

Henry (*satisfied, moving away from her*) I thought so. (*He looks at his brief again*) Now—if I could think of something equally good for Bernard . . . (*He sits to work on his brief*)

Katherine (*rising, outraged*) Aren't you ashamed?

Henry (*working*) What?

Katherine Ashamed!

Henry What of?

Katherine Of what you've done to Sam.

Henry What've I done to Sam?

Katherine Corrupted him.

Astonished, he puts down his brief and looks at her

Henry (*after a pause*) I thought he was supposed to do that to me.

Katherine He didn't have a chance, did he? He's too simple . . . Too full of faith!

Henry Faith? Who are you talking about, exactly?

Katherine You know . . . (*She sits on the sofa*)

Henry Not the Sacred Saint Samuel and All Angels? The Blessed Martyr Brown of the Bronx? I'm sorry, I didn't recognize him for a moment.

Katherine You wouldn't understand. He believed, in everything.

Henry And when did he convert you? All those little lunches, I suppose at the Trattoria in Belsize Park?

Katherine We never went out to lunch. He used to bring things here. From the delicatessen. Wonderful things! Russian salad and pastrami on rye and strawberry cheesecake and coffee in little plastic cups with lids on them to keep it warm. He used to bring it in a carrier bag. Why don't you ever do that?

Henry I'm sorry.

Katherine And we'd sit here. Over there. Where you're sitting.

Henry gets up and moves

And he'd be caring so hard his forehead would be damp, gleaming with sweat and he'd have to undo his tie as if he were being strangled . . .

Henry Was he caring about anything in particular?

Katherine Of course he was! About the Bomb and Suez and the Generation Gap and how he never communicated with his Father and the End of the World . . .

Henry The End of the World has always seemed the least of our worries.

Katherine And about me! That's not one of your worries, either?

Henry I wish I'd known . . .

Katherine You carefully avoided finding out.

Henry I could've given him something constructive to worry about. Like the rates . . . (*Pause. He goes back to work*) There's one thing . . .

Katherine What?

Henry About Sam . . .

Katherine Let's stop talking about him, shall we?

Henry All right. (*He is bored with his brief and goes to the radiogram*) Do you want some music?

Katherine No.

Henry We will now stand in silent prayer to mark the passing of Mr Samuel Brown . . . (*Pause. Katherine does not answer*) He hasn't rung up?

Katherine No.

Henry Or written to you at all?

Katherine No. Of course not.

Henry I must say I think's that a bloody cheek.

Katherine Do you?

Henry I certainly do. All that caring and sweating and loosening his collar at you over the pastrami sandwiches and one little setback and he's off like a bloody butterfly. He's probably up the street—caring about the physiotherapist next door. (*Pause. She does not react*) Do you miss him?

There is the sound of a very small child calling from upstairs

Katherine Not particularly. (*She looks at him*) Do you? It seems you didn't settle her at all!

Katherine goes up the stairs
    There is a ring at the front door. Henry answers it and lets in a reluctant and shamefaced Sam Brown, who is carrying a potted plant

Sam You're going to let me in?
Henry We were just wondering where you'd got to.
Sam You were? Both of you?
Henry Of course.
Sam I brought this . . .
Henry Katherine'll like that. She's just up with the children . . .
Sam For you, Henry. I know you like the home to look nice. Well, I couldn't think of a present . . .

Henry takes the plant

    You're not offended?
Henry Not at all. It was very—thoughtful. (*He puts it on the mantelpiece*)
Sam I had to come round. I had to apologize—heartfelt . . . I expect you can guess. I've gone in for a bit of self examination. Painful—painful process.
Henry I don't know. I've always found it a lot better than examining other people.
Sam I said to myself, "Sam Brown," I said, "I hope you're proud of what you've done. Oh boy, I surely hope you're proud."
Henry Well, you certainly got further than anyone else I've ever known on a pastrami sandwich.
Sam (*pained*) Henry. Please . . .
Henry I'm sorry.
Sam This hasn't been easy for me. I'd like you to respect that.
Henry I'm very sorry.
Sam A friend! An actual friend. That's what makes it—so hard to forgive myself. You know, Hank, I've lived around, naturally. I got laid in many quarters of the globe . . .
Henry You're referring to your sexual experiences, naturally—and not the circumstances of your birth?
Sam Henry!
Henry It always sounds so like being hatched out. I really am sorry. What do you want me to say? Congratulations.
Sam (*patiently*) I would like you, Henry, just to try and understand . . .
Henry I will try. I promise . . .
Sam I have had broads—from the age of ten on. Well, a man loses count after a while.
Henry I wish I could.
Sam What?
Henry Lose count. If only they could merge into one anonymous broad. It's the bloody individuality . . .

Sam But this is what I thought. No-one is worth trading for a friend. We had found friendship, Henry. Working together, fighting, making it up, getting to know all each other's little faults and weaknesses . . . Of course, it hasn't been long.

Henry Really? It felt as though it was just coming up to our golden wedding . . .

Sam That's right, man! That is absolutely correct. Surpasses the love of woman. (*He puts an arm round him*)

Henry (*moving away*) Excuse me . . .

Sam Like the Bible says, old chum. It surpasses the love of woman. Don't be English—man.

Henry What?

Sam Don't be bloody English. We are just a little bit more open about this where I come from. A little less easily shocked? A little more psycho-analytically oriented may be . . .

Henry I'd love to know what you're talking about.

Sam With us it may be a little more common. You know what is in constant use with us? Packaged foods. All sort of packaged and frozen chicken con carne and suchlike. Well, boy—have these chickens been jammed packed full of hormones! Male and female, both—just packed in at random.

Henry Sam . . .

Sam Henry . . . ?

Henry I'm really quite pleased to see you and thank you for the flowers— but can you tell me what any of this has to do with the hormones in chickens.

Sam Well . . . some of our guys are getting a little less like guys than they used to be. I could see that our friendship meant a good deal to you. Katherine has no right to come between us. A woman's love is not so pure. It hasn't got the strength—and the generosity. What did the old Arab do?

Henry I don't know, Sam. Is it going to be a joke?

Sam His friend admired his wife—so he offered the wife to the friend, Henry Winter. You made me ashamed. In a friendship like ours. Women just don't enter into it.

Henry Don't they? I suppose they don't.

Sam They just don't enter in. Friends . . . That's what counts. (*He holds out his hands*) And the project!

Henry And the project. (*He shakes Sam's hand*)

Sam The project still means a lot to me. You don't mind my coming round here again? For work sessions . . . Well, it's better than an office.

Henry Be my guest—I'm sorry.

Sam Henry. I have another small favour to ask you. If you want to kick me out after I've said this—well, I guess I had it coming.

Henry This isn't . . . something to do with the old Arab?

Sam Not at all! The fact is—I'm kinda between apartments at the moment. I had this wonderful place in Soho Square all set up and then this schmuck got married and—of course I could go to a hotel . . .

Henry (*smiling, welcoming*) I wouldn't dream of it.

Sam I have acquaintances, of course, but not real friends like you and Katherine . . .

Henry Be my . . . I'm sorry. Of course. You can sleep on the sofa.

Katherine comes in from upstairs. She sees Sam

Katherine Well.

Sam (*awkward and guilty*) Hullo, there! Long time no see.

Katherine You did leave rather suddenly.

Sam Katherine . . .

Katherine Of course, my husband has a remarkable talent for seeing people off the premises. He usually manages to get us left entirely alone.

She moves towards the exotic potted plant she has noticed

Sam I'm sorry. I called round to say I was sorry. To make—some sort of amends, I guess . . .

Katherine Well, Sam. That's very nice of you. It's beautiful.

Henry (*firmly*) It's mine. (*He moves in front of the plant*)

Katherine What?

Henry Sam brought that floral tribute, as a personal present for me. Katherine—I think you'd better find some blankets.

Katherine Have you gone mad?

Henry I have invited Sam to be—to stay with us for a little while. It seems he's had a little bad luck. He's fallen between flats.

Katherine (*looking at them both with amused amazement*) Good God! When's the wedding . . . ?

Sam What?

Katherine (*to Henry*) When's the happy day? I mean, first he brings you flowers—then you tell me he's moving in.

Henry What's the matter? Jealous?

Katherine You're taking him over!

Henry Sam and I just happen to have something rather fine going for us. Surpassing the love of women . . .

Katherine (*to Sam*) You're not going to let him do it?

Sam Do what?

Katherine Have you to live in. As a mother's help!

Sam (*with dignity*) I really don't know what you're suggesting, Katherine. I thought I'd move in here so I could get down to work with Henry.

Henry If you've got any strong objection . . .

Katherine Don't let me come between you.

Henry Sam just thought it'd be convenient.

Katherine Convenient. For you. I suppose so.

Henry For the work, naturally. (*He moves to Sam and gives him a brisk slap on the back*) Well, old chum. Feel like a work session, do you?

Sam Ready when you are, feller.

Katherine (*raising her eyes to heaven*) Oh, my God!

Henry What're you going to do, Katherine?

Katherine What do you suggest? Do you two boys want to be left alone together?

Sam No. No, of course not . . .

Henry Not necessarily.

Katherine Well, then. I'll just hang around doing something feminine. (*She looks around the room for something to do*) I'll water the plant . . .

Katherine goes into the kitchen

Sam (*lying back on the sofa and kicking off his shoes*) I have been thinking about the project. Pretty hard in the last few days. I feel—our married couple need something.

Henry No doubt about it.

Sam Maybe—an extra problem.

Katherine enters with a milk bottle containing green washing-up liquid shaken up in it

Katherine An extra problem! That's it. For the couple who have everything. (*She waters the plant, drowning it*)

Henry That shouldn't be too hard. What sort of problem would you suggest?

Sam A modern problem . . . Something to give this story a rather contemporary look. (*Pause*) Oh, my God—inspiration!

Katherine It's struck again? (*She sits*)

Sam (*to Henry*) Look! I wouldn't want to force anything on you, kid, and it's your story, anyway, but suppose—I mean, just suppose we kick this one around a little—I can speak freely in front of you, Katherine?

Katherine I thought you already had.

Sam Thanks. Well, just suppose this man—this husband in our story—had to face with a great deal of courage. And good taste, of course. The human problem of sexual inversion.

Katherine (*singing*) "Here I go again
                        I hear the trumpets blow again . . ."

Sam Of course, it would have to be tastefully done.

Katherine You mean he's a faggot, Samuel?

Sam Doesn't that have a certain truthfulness?

Katherine I should say so.

Sam And her problem is—she feels it her duty to live with a man who is otherwise orientated sexwise, quite frankly.

Katherine Why does she feel it her duty?

Sam Well, why don't we say . . . Got it! For the sake of the kids!

Katherine Brilliant!

Sam Now we are cooking. Doesn't that give her a real dilemma? And warmth. You know what this wife needs?

Katherine What does she need?

Sam A friend! A sympathetic friend . . . Say a guy—who knows her really

well. I mean, he's really got the hots for her but she's married to a man
he greatly respects . . . and well. He keeps his distance . . .

Katherine I'll get you some blankets. (*She moves to go out of the room*)
Sounds very moving.

Sam Doesn't it. I'm glad you think so, Katherine. (*He gets up and starts
to follow her*) We've got something going for us now. A purity—a kind
of nobility, even! Want some help?

Katherine exits upstairs

You know—with a warm dilemma like that we might even get a "yes"
from Deborah Kerr.

Sam goes out after Katherine

The phone rings. Henry picks it up

Henry Miss Griffin? Well . . . Hullo, Miss Griffin darling . . . (*He looks
round the room*) It's not all that easy actually . . . Visitors? Yes . . .
Tomorrow. I'll be there at nine . . . For a nice chat in the cells . . . No
. . . No, I'm sorry. Of course I can't get out tonight. Well . . . It's im-
possible. Not for a long time, I'm afraid. You see. It's happened . . .
Total war! Yes. Daniel told her. (*He whispers*) The gas oven!

Katherine comes back with an armful of blankets. Sam follows with pillows

(*Beginning to talk quickly*) If we could get Bernard's prints on the gas
oven we could prove he wasn't at the scene of the crime at all. He was
at home with his mother—heating up the steak and mushroom pie.
Look into it, will you? (*He puts down the phone*)

Sam Has he got an alibi?

Henry Always. (*He gets up and moves to the table*) It's always possible,
given a little ingenuity, to prove that you were in two places at any given
moment.

Katherine starts to make up a bed on the sofa

I'm hungry.

Katherine Then why don't you cook us a cosy little snack before we tuck
Sam up for the night?

Henry goes into the kitchen

(*Sitting on the pouffe*) I'm sorry. He's treating you very badly.

Sam He's being great. It's great of him to have me here. (*He continues
with the bed-making*) Say what you like about Henry. He behaved like
a gentleman.

Katherine That's right. Badly.

Sam What did you mean by that—"mother's help"?

Katherine He's got you, hasn't he, exactly where he wants you?

Sam Where's that?

Katherine Here. Doing the tough work. That's what he's always recommended—as a solution for every problem. "Get a man in."

Sam I behaved badly. I blame myself—very much.

Katherine "Get a man in." To mend the Hoover and put washers on taps and provide his wife with a bit of an alternative to *Listen with Mother* . . .

Sam And when I came back not a word of blame. Not a word!

Katherine Or even to do the real dirty jobs—like saving my life.

Sam Like what?

Katherine Not a great life saver, our Henry. Shall I tell you a scene? You might be able to use it.

Sam Go on. Shoot. We're really creative tonight, aren't we?

Katherine I was thinking—of a scene with the children. Perhaps—somewhere on holiday.

Sam Kids! That's good.

Katherine (*ignoring him*) On some huge white beach. In England. With the children swimming. Teeth chattering. Gooseflesh. Swimming, determined.

Sam And what's he doing?

Katherine What's he always doing? Cooking!

Sam Making a fire of driftwood on the sand. Frying sausages. The way the kids like it.

Katherine He's got a cook's hat on, maybe—and a striped apron.

Sam Don't be ridiculous!

Katherine And one of the children . . .

Sam One of his?

Katherine One of theirs. Is shouting. Calling from the water. There's a tide on that beach, you see. It pulls you out however hard you swim against it. He never asked about it, he never discovered. He was busy cooking. Anyway, this child is screaming, being carried away. Drowning . . .

Sam I like it.

Katherine Extraordinarily quickly.

Sam I can see it. In visual terms. We shoot down—and this kid's face is actually under the water. We shoot through water. I can see it all!

Katherine So could he! He saw a man—far out to sea. In the direction this child was floating. "Let him save her", he said. "He's much nearer to her than I am." Get a man in.

Sam Katherine, you make me ashamed.

Katherine You?

Sam I ran out on you. That night . . .

Katherine He made you.

Sam It's just that I couldn't do it. To a sensitive guy like Henry.

Katherine Sensitive? He's about as sensitive as a ten-ton truck. Bashing on his way—regardless.

Sam (*moving nearer to her*) Katherine. Sweet Katherine . . .

Katherine Yes?

Sam I want to fuck you.

As Sam is speaking Henry comes in from the kitchen

Henry Anyone want a cheese on toast?
Katherine Sam just said, "I want to fuck you".
Sam It's a great line. Don't you think so? For the script I mean.
Henry Oh, for the script. Brilliant. And so original.
Sam Why not be original? Why not say "fuck"?
Henry I've been saying that as long as I can remember
Sam But not on the movies, Hank. Don't you see the distinction?
Katherine Do we have to?
Sam What?
Katherine Do we actually *have* to say it?
Sam (*thinking it over*) Well, you don't *have* to. But it'd be kind of nice if
     you did.
Katherine Can't we use that word for it they used to use in the Golden
     Oldies of Movieland?
Sam What word is that, Katherine?
Katherine "Dance."
Sam Sorry. I'm not with you . . .
Henry Dance. Samuel, where were you brought up, exactly? (*He sings
     suddenly*) "I'm dancing with tears in my eyes
              Because the girl in my arms isn't you."
Katherine   "Say that I will always dance
              The anniversary dance with you . . ."
Henry   "They're dancing overhead
              Up above my lonely bed."

*Henry starts a tap dance, and as she sings Katherine joins in till they are
doing, for Sam's benefit, their long-practised version of Fred Astaire and
Ginger Rogers*

Katherine   "I love my ceiling more
              Since it is a dancing floor . . ."
Henry   "I won't dance
              How could I?
              I won't dance, why should I?
              I won't dance, Madame, with you.
              My heart won't let my feet do what they want to . . .
Katherine   "When you dance you're sweet and you are gent . . . le
              Especially when you do the CON . . . TIN . . . ENT . . . AL."
Henry   "It's heaven sent . . . le
              And sentiment . . . le
              Heaven . . .
              I'm in heaven . . .

              I won't dance
              How could I?
              I won't dance. Why should I?
              I won't dance, Madame, with you . . .

They finish the dance in a fine pirouette and, holding hands, bow to Sam who starts, reluctantly, to clap. He goes on clapping. Katherine and Henry exit upstairs

Sam takes off his shoes, trousers and jacket and gets into bed on the sofa. He is instantly asleep. The Lights fade to a Black-Out

When the Lights come up again it is daylight. Sam is lying in a heap of blankets. The sound is heard of the children who have visited him earlier. The doorbell rings. Sam rises and staggers out to the kitchen. The doorbell rings again. There is the sound of a tap running, then Sam returns and goes towards the front door. The bell rings again as he reaches it and opens it

Griselda enters

Sam gets quickly behind the open door

Griselda Have I come to the right house?
Sam The right house for what?
Griselda (*coming into the room*) I wanted to see Mrs Winter. It's rather urgent.
Sam Katherine . . . ?

Katherine enters downstairs

Katherine Sam. You look terrible. What time did the children get at you?
Sam Around four, I guess. Look, there's someone . . .
Griselda Mrs Winter. I had to come and talk to you. Urgently.
Sam (*picking up his clothes*) I'll go. I was just fixing myself a glass of kiddies' orange drink . . .

Sam exits to the kitchen

Katherine (*calling after him*) There's some Delrosa rose hip syrup if you like it better. (*To Griselda*) I'm sorry. Our lodger seems to have over-slept . . .
Griselda (*who has been looking at her*) You look different.
Katherine Different from what?
Griselda Different from what I expected. You didn't mind my coming?
Katherine No. Should I? (*She gathers the sheets and blankets together and puts them on the back of the sofa*)
Griselda Henry told me a bit last night. And then this morning. We were having coffee—down at the Old Bailey.
Katherine Henry?
Griselda Your husband, Henry.
Katherine Oh, *that* Henry . . .
Griselda He told me it all. I just got up and left. Mr Fidella'll have to look after the case—I couldn't stay. I had to set your mind at rest, you see— I had to tell you it's all over. Finished. Completely. With me and Henry. (*Pause*) You'll never do that again, Mrs Winter, will you . . . ?

Katherine Excuse me—this may sound awfully rude but—who are you, exactly?

Griselda I'm Griselda—Griselda Griffin. I used to go out with Henry.

Katherine Gristle! My husband actually took you out?

Griselda Well, not *very* much.

Katherine Four-thirty. The Kardomah, Fleet Street. Did he stand you tea? I mean, let's face it, my husband can be bloody mean.

Griselda (*with a faint smile*) I managed to winkle a cake out of him occasionally.

Katherine The bastard! Didn't he ever buy you dinner?

Griselda Well—once.

Katherine The menu at the Carvery? All you can get on your plate for twelve-and-six?

Griselda You'd taken the children to stay with his mother in the country. You weren't due back till ten. We had to leave before the sweet trolley . . .

Katherine I can only apologize for my husband. He's got the most despicable manners.

Griselda Oh, it's not your fault. Nothing's your fault, Mrs Winter.

Katherine Please. Katherine.

Griselda All right then. Katherine. I'm so ashamed. About that night.

Katherine What night, exactly?

Griselda The night I came round with my nightie in a bag.

Pause

Katherine You came round with *what*?

Griselda In a paper bag. He'd never seen me in any night wear.

Katherine Of course! That night.

Griselda (*after a pause*) What really is unforgivable is—involving the children! Of course that little child told you. He had every right to tell you. He was protecting himself, that's all. I was a challenge. I realize that. To the whole family stability. (*Pause*) Wasn't I?

Katherine (*reassuringly*) Of course you were, dear! A tremendous challenge.

Griselda If—if my child told me he saw a strange woman coming up the stairs with a ridiculous orange nylon slumber wear—which she'd brought in a carrier bag—I'd do it, too.

Katherine Do what, too?

Griselda Put my head in the gas oven.

Katherine Is that what I did?

Griselda nods miserably. Pause. Katherine looks at her

Are you sure that's what I did?

Griselda Sure.

Katherine So let's get this perfectly straight, Griselda. You came round—with your things in a carrier bag.

Griselda Only because you'd left home. He told me that . . .

Katherine Oh, I see. I'd left home.

Griselda With a film producer.

Katherine And Daniel saw you. Why did you leave?

Griselda Because you were coming back. You'd decided to give your marriage another chance. And I've ruined it all! Ruined! I was there, you see—going upstairs. That's the point.

Katherine And Daniel passed on—all that information?

Griselda Didn't he?

Pause

Katherine No.

Griselda But you knew about it?

Katherine Yes.

Griselda Then who told you?

Katherine You.

Griselda What?

Katherine You did. You just have.

Griselda Oh, Mrs Winter! Where've I got myself?

Katherine I have absolutely no idea. I must say it's fascinating.

Griselda What must you think of me?

Katherine Another of my husband's works of fiction.

Griselda Then what was he talking about?

Katherine Who can ever tell?

Griselda He told me—war had broken out. He seemed so, terribly concerned!

Katherine Then he was lying. He's never concerned about the truth.

Griselda Are you going to tell him—I came round?

Katherine I don't think so. He'd be so flattered.

Griselda Flattered?

Katherine Two women. Saying terrible things about him. I don't think he deserves that pleasure, do you?

Griselda I don't—really understand . . .

Katherine Be grateful. You'll never have to. I wish I'd known, dear. What you were going through. I'd have been round to beg your forgiveness.

Griselda To forgive *you* . . . ?

Katherine For Henry. He shouldn't be let out alone.

Griselda You've been so lovely. I never expected—you'd be so gentle.

Katherine smiles at her, steps forward, and kisses her

Katherine I hope we can be friends, at least.

Griselda So do I. (*She starts to go*)

Katherine What about tea, sometime, in the Kardomah?

Griselda You're joking!

Katherine No, Griselda, dear, I never joke.

Griselda goes

Katherine stands a moment looking after her. Then she folds the blankets and puts them at the end of the sofa

Sam comes out of the kitchen, a tumbler of some pink drink in his hand

I'm glad you like the Rose Hip.
Sam It's incredible!
Katherine The children like it.
Sam What that girl said. What *about* that?
Katherine You heard it?
Sam The door was open and . . .
Katherine That's the worst of this house. It's like living on a stage.
Sam Incredible!
Katherine No, it's not. Once you get to know Henry . . .
Sam You think he actually told her . . . all that?
Katherine Once you get to know my husband you'll believe anything.
Sam He told her all that . . . nonsense, about *you.*
Katherine He has to make me responsible, you see. For everything.

Katherine goes upstairs with the blankets

Sam stands for a moment, the glass in his hand, then picks up his shoes

Henry enters through the front door with his brief-case

Henry Isn't a bit early? To start on the wine?
Sam It's rose hip syrup.
Henry How revolting!
Sam (*putting down the glass*) You're back early. (*He sits to put on his shoes*)
Henry The case finished—rather unexpectedly. Tell me—you haven't seen someone—from my solicitor's office?

Katherine comes down the stairs

Sam Yes, she was here.
Henry Oh.
Katherine Gristle was here. Fascinating! (*Coming into the room*) You're back early.
Henry Yes.
Katherine Did you lose the case?
Henry No. No, not really. It was rather funny, as a matter of fact.
Katherine Just for once—couldn't you do something that's not funny?
Henry We happened to have hit, Bernard and I, on the opening day of the Old Bailey—one of those quaint ceremonies which make law so lovable and lend such a touch of gaiety to a ten-year stretch. Bernard came up from the cells, blinking like a mole, to be greeted by the sight of a scarlet-ermine-trimmed judge, sniffing his nosegay, being bowed into place by lots of gentlemen in lace ruffles and swords. Apparently he mistook number one court for heaven and shouted "Hallelujah. I have passed over. The Day of Judgement is at hand. They made a hospital order. (*He laughs*)

Katherine I don't think that's funny.

Henry (*dead-pan*) No. It's not funny, really—quite a reasonable hospital order.

Sam The Day of Judgement! I should think it is. As far as you're concerned.

Henry He'll probably be out for Christmas.

Sam Your Day of Judgement. I should imagine it's just about due. What did you tell that Miss Griffin?

Katherine (*to Sam*) You don't understand Henry.

Sam I certainly don't.

Katherine He just isn't capable of a plain straightforward brush off. I mean, he couldn't even bring himself to say, "Miss Griffin, darling, you bore me", or "Don't ring me, I'll ring you", or "I've met something strange and new from the typing pool and I'll be having tea in Joe Lyons in future". He wants everyone to go on loving him.

Sam So?

Katherine So he puts on his best tragic expression and says, "Don't ring me, darling, because whenever you do . . . my wife prepares for immolation!"

Sam You bastard! What've you given that girl? What sort of a hell of a load of responsibility?

Henry Responsibility? What for?

Sam Tragedy. Could've been . . .

Henry Could've been? Could've been farce.

Sam What the hell did you let her believe . . .?

Henry Anyway. Something interesting.

Sam What?

Henry Not dull. At least it wasn't dull. What we told her.

Katherine "We?" Don't drag me into it. He has to bring everything home. Didn't I tell you?

Henry What did you bring home?

Katherine What?

Henry Him!

Sam Me?

Henry Not good enough for you, was it? Not a secret little romance among the paper cups and pastrami sandwiches. You had to make a great announcement! A great scene. You had to drag me into it.

Sam Is that right, Katherine?

Pause. Katherine does not answer

(*To Henry*) I guess she wanted to try me out—she wanted to watch my reactions.

Henry No. She wanted to watch mine.

Sam Katherine!

Pause. Again she does not answer

I was another one, uh? Someone to provide a little dramatic material for both of you! I suppose you think you've given me something which isn't exactly dull. You know what you gave me? Something so damn complicated I couldn't understand a word of it! (*To Katherine*) I wanted to make a grab for you. A plain simple grab to which any man's entitled. And before I knew it you'd got me all confused with lies and stories and "I don't want her, you have her", and "No, I didn't mean that really . . ." And now I see what it was all for. A present for me. Gift wrapped. Uh? Something for me to remember in the long years ahead when we carve our Sunday roast and cook apple pie and pay our mortgages. The glorious, fascinating days when we tangled with the Winters. Dicing with death. Jam packed with thrills and spills. Is that what we're supposed to remember? You know what I think you are? A couple of monsters. (*He sits*)

Henry Not monsters. Just married.

Katherine It makes it difficult, for anyone who comes near us.

Henry It makes it much more difficult for us.

Sam (*looking at them*) Well—well—well! Oh, God, I'm sorry for you! I'm sorry you spend so much on wine and little bottles of herbs and casserole dishes and you can't afford the gas. I'm sorry you've got about nineteen kids upstairs who're just about too grown up to join in your games any more. And that includes the baby! I'm sorry you find each other so unsatisfactory that you have to grab people in off the sidewalk for laughs or kicks or whatever the hell it is. I'm sorry for you both. I'm sorry . . .

Henry Very good speech, Sam. (*To Katherine*) Wouldn't you say so? Eloquent.

Sam What do I have—did you say Mr laugh-a-minute Henry Winter? "Three D emotions?" "Feelings in gorgeous technicolor?" Want to swap? Or are you happy with no feelings at all? Feelings you took out and looked at and made jokes about so often that they've sort of faded out and died, haven't they, old chum?

Henry Where did you say you came from?

Sam What the hell does it matter where I came from?

Katherine You came out of nowhere. We didn't ask you. You came here to take us over.

Sam Big chance! Like a small bicycle repair shop making a bid for General Motors.

Katherine You hear what he called us? He called us General Motors!

Henry Eloquent! Sam Brown has become eloquent. (*Pause*) There's something in what he says.

Katherine I told you. If you let him in here he'd corrupt us . . .

Henry The children are much older than we are. I see in their eyes, as I settle them down for the night, looks of remote disapproval.

Katherine (*to Sam*) You should have left us alone.

Sam I only wanted you to work. That's all I had, a job of work for you.

Katherine Is *that* why you came?

Sam You agreed to do it! You took on this assignment. You have a certain responsibility. To the project.

Henry The show must go on?

Katherine Why?

Sam How much work have you done lately? How many pages?

Henry I've been busy. Rather—occupied.

Sam Amusing yourself with attempted murder! You have neglected my story.

Katherine He's right, you know. After all, you took Sam on . . .

Henry *I* took him on . . . ?

Sam A person can't rely on you, Henry.

Katherine I agree.

Henry What?

Katherine I agree—he's not to be relied on. (*To Sam*) You put out a hand for him—and he's not there. It's like a sudden gap in the staircase and under it—a great, great fall—black nothing . . .

Henry (*to Katherine*) And *you're* so dependable, of course!

Katherine More dependable.

Henry Like when I was here alone. All alone—looking after the kids and you came back and announced your forthcoming marriage—to this— this visitor!

Katherine All alone! Only with about ten girls running around with half Neatawear in paper bags.

Henry You didn't know that! You absolutely weren't to know. (*Pause*) I couldn't depend on you.

Katherine You're pathetic! If you want to depend on me you'd find me much more dependable.

Henry If I didn't want to depend on you I wouldn't care if you were dependable or not.

Sam (*shouting at both of them*) Oh, for God's sake! We've got to find a resolution.

Pause

Henry What?

Katherine Would you like to suggest one?

Sam What we really require here—is something upbeat! I mean it's got to be hopeful.

Katherine Are you actually proposing, Sam, a happy ending . . . ?

Sam A happy ending. With a twist, if possible. Now what would that *be* exactly?

Katherine Divorce.

Sam Oh, come on, Katherine.

Katherine A happy ending—for them both.

Henry And apparently for everyone else around.

Katherine That's it! For everyone, unfortunately around.

Sam Oh, come on! You're kidding! Divorce? Divorce has got to be sad. Divorce is failure, isn't it? I mean it's by its nature—gloomy.

Katherine Gloomier than marriage?

Sam Hey, kids. What're you trying to tell me? You're trying to tell me there's a twist—are you? Wait a minute. I'm starting to get it . . . A loving divorce! A really meaningful divorce. With love. Do you suppose an audience might identify? Look. These two love each other. Let's say. They're crazy for each other. But they can't stop knocking the hell out of each other. So they end up having a loving divorce. Out of compassion. Done with taste. Have I got it?

Katherine I don't know.

The Lights fade to a Black-Out. Katherine exits to the kitchen; Henry through the arch; Sam sits below the fire and takes out a buff-coloured script

As the Lights come up again, to evening, Katherine enters from the kitchen with an armful of Henry's shirts, packaged fresh from the laundry, and Henry comes in with a suitcase. They meet in the middle of the room and Henry drops the case, open on the floor. Katherine drops the shirts into the case

Henry How many?

Katherine Twelve! A man with twelve shirts and no moral principles.

Henry (*crouching by the case, arranging the shirts*) Fifteen.

Katherine What?

Henry I own fifteen.

Katherine Three are in the wash.

Henry Then I can't go.

Katherine I'll bring them round on Saturday.

Henry No! You won't bring them round. I'm not seeing you again, Katherine. Not ever.

Katherine (*with a shrug*) Just as you like.

Henry (*shutting the case and standing up*) I want to find myself.

Sam (*nodding approvingly*) That's good!

Katherine (*looking at him, astonished*) You like that?

Sam "Find myself." That's very good.

Katherine I think it's ludicrous! As though he'd left himself in a taxi and was just popping round to the Lost Property Office. (*She goes to the table, picks up a typescript and looks through it*) What comes next? (*She finds her place in the script*) "When you're gone I'll have that crack in the plaster mended." (*She looks at Henry, puzzled*)

Henry (*pointing to a chipped and damaged corner of the wall*) The plaster.

Katherine When you're gone I'll have that crack in the plaster mended.

Henry Why don't you keep it as it is? As a memento of the great attack! Put poppies round it and observe two minutes' bloody silence . . .

Katherine What attack?

Henry Your attack!

Katherine *Mine?*

Henry (*moving to the wall*) This is where an Italian lamp, constructed from a pile of ceramic lemons, and bought with the proceeds from my first play for steam radio to add a new element of Theatrical High Camp to our lives, was flung at my head. And it's no credit to your marksmanship that my brains weren't spattered all over the John Barnes haircord.

Katherine (*putting down the typescript and starting to laugh*) Miss Griffin!
Henry "John Barnes haircord." What an impossible line!
Katherine (*laughing*) Miss Griselda Griffin!
Sam (*puzzled*) Is that in the script?
Katherine No! Gristle never made the script. She was more of a noise off, actually.
Henry Look. Shall we get on with it?
Sam (*quietly, patiently*) We're here to work, Katherine.
Katherine Yes, of course, Sam. Of course that's why we're here. (*She looks through the script again, speaks to Henry*) Do you have to go?
Henry (*moving to the door with the case*) You know I have to.
Katherine Why? (*She moves to him*)
Henry I suppose—we care too much . . .
Katherine I know.
Henry We're stifling each other, choking each other to death. We have to move away so we can breathe.
Sam That's great!
Katherine Our divorce will be an occasion for mutual concern.
Henry And tenderness.

Sam, watching, covers his eyes

Katherine And respect . . .
Henry A lifelong and loving separation.
Katherine We can be ourselves . . .
Henry And not each other.

They are close together, reading the script

Katherine Can we—do you think we can make it?
Henry We can try. All I can say is . . . (*Also making a heroic effort to say it seriously*) Good luck, Katherine! (*He moves tragically to the door, starting to shake with laughter*)
Katherine Go now, darling. Go quickly. (*She manages to say this, then throws the script down on the table*) It's ridiculous!
Henry (*moving back towards her*) Absurd.
Katherine It'll never do. It'll never—never do. (*She looks at Sam who is still sitting with his hand over his face*) What's happened to Sam?

They both move on either side of Sam, looking at him. He does not uncover his face

Henry Sam. What's the matter?
Katherine (*kneeling beside him, concerned*) Samuel. Samovitch.
Henry (*also kneeling*) Courage, M'sieur Brun.
Katherine Sam Brown. What's oop?
Henry Brown, Braun, Brunovitch.
Katherine Oh, my God! I believe he's deeply moved. (*She moves Sam's head, looks at his face, incredulous*) Tears! Real, actual, genuine tears.
Henry (*amazed*) Brunowski's weeping!

Sam dries his eyes, blows his nose and embraces them both

Sam I love you. I love you both.
Katherine He's crying—and he loves us.
Sam I knew you could do it. I knew you kids could do it. The first time I walked in that door!

Sam rises, takes the script and walks towards the front door. Katherine and Henry rise with him. Henry opens the front door

I'm going to see—if there's anything I can do with this. Don't ring me.
Henry Do you think, you might be able to find us, a little finance?
Sam You two seem to think about nothing but finance! Think about art for a change.

Sam goes

Henry shuts the front door and walks back into the room

Henry "If there's anything he can do with it."

Katherine gathers up the pillows from the sofa

Our lives! Do you think he'll do anything with it?
Katherine I don't know. He seems determined . . . (*She starts to go up the stairs*)
Henry You mean he cares?
Katherine (*disappearing upstairs*) Well. At least we can get this room tidied up.

Katherine goes

Henry moves quickly to the telephone and dials

Miss Griffin? . . . It was a good result, wasn't it? A pretty good result . . . Look, I don't know what Katherine told you, but——

Katherine comes downstairs

—she says some improbable things, you know. Some quite unreliable things. For her own—purposes. (*He puts down the phone slowly*)

Katherine watches him

Katherine What did she do? Ring off? Before you could say good-bye? (*She ruffles the cushions on the sofa and sits*) Well, that's Gristle gone.
Henry And Mr Brown?
Katherine Yes. He's gone.
Henry Do you miss him? And Bernice. I didn't tell you.
Katherine What?
Henry Bernice is dead. I never told you. (*He sits beside her on the sofa*) Bernice! Of all people . . .
Katherine We look like being all on our own.
Henry Yes. It seems rather quiet. Without old Samuel. And without Bernard.

Katherine Who?

Henry Bernard Duffield.

Katherine Oh, yes. The Day of Judgement . . .

Henry It never comes, actually, does it?

Katherine It's come.

Henry What?

Katherine Now and for ever. We'll go on paying for it.

Henry Paying for what exactly?

Katherine The day you walked up the garden path. In those bloody deceptive gum boots.

Henry You're wrong, you know. I wasn't even wearing gum boots.

Katherine Am I—am I really mistaken?

The children are heard calling

Children (*off*) Mummy . . . ! Daddy . . . !

Henry (*shouting up at the ceiling*) Leave us alone! We're not doing anything wrong! (*To Katherine*) So—puritanical—those children! They were perfectly ordinary, crêpe-soled, suede-topped, elastic-sided hush puppies!

Katherine (*looking at him, bleakly*) One day, just for a change—why don't you try telling me the truth?

They are looking at each other, as—

the CURTAIN *falls*

FURNITURE AND PROPERTY LIST

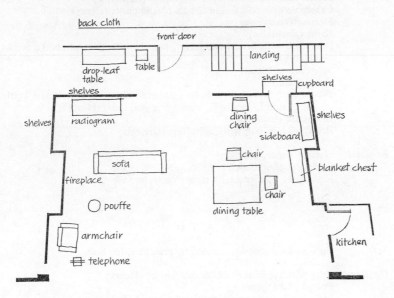

ACT I

On stage: Sofa. *On it:* cushions
Armchair
3 dining chairs
Pouffe
Radiogram and records
Sideboard. *In it:* candlestick with candle, broken candlestick, loose candles, paper napkins, glasses, plates, cutlery
Large table. *On it:* typewriter, paper, legal briefs, dying pot plant, bills, empty bottles, children's toys
2 occasional tables (in passage)
On floor and furniture generally: toys, children's clothes and nursery paraphernalia including baby's potty, and doll under table
Over mantelpiece: mirror
On shelves: books, hidden packet of cigarettes, hidden black address book
On walls: children's drawings, photographs, posters
On floor below fire: telephone, pad and pencil
On floor by sideboard: waste-paper basket with empty wine bottle
Practical plug for fire, Hoover and kettle

Electric fire with plastic coals
Carpet
Stair carpet

Off stage: Elaborate table lamp (**Henry**)
Hairbrush and towel (**Katherine**)
Old Chianti bottle (**Henry**)
Plastic baby bath with washing things (**Katherine**)
Casserole dish containing child's plastic pants (**Henry**)
Hoover (**Katherine**)
Knife (**Katherine**)
Brief-case with briefs, typescript, pencils, bills, several child's bricks
(**Henry**)
Screwdriver (**Sam**)
Script (**Sam**)
Plastic bath with baby's bottle, nappies, alarm clock, electric kettle
(full), tin of Ostermilk, measuring jug, ladle (**Henry**)
Brief-case (**Griselda**)
Brown carrier bag with nightdress (**Griselda**)

Personal: **Henry:** watch, latchkey
Sam: matches, watch
Katherine: handbag with empty cigarette case

ACT II

Set: Buff-covered script concealed by armchair, for **Sam**

Off stage: Tray with remains of children's supper (**Henry**)
Potted plant (**Sam**)
Milk bottle containing washing-up liquid (**Katherine**)
Blankets (**Katherine**)
Pillows (**Sam**)
Tumbler of pink drink (**Sam**)
Pile of laundered shirts (**Katherine**)
Suitcase (**Henry**)

LIGHTING PLOT

Property fittings required: wall-brackets or pendant, elaborate table lamp, electric fire with plastic coals
Interior. A living-room. The same scene throughout

ACT I. Night

To open: Artificial lighting on. Fire lit

Cue 1	**Henry** plugs in lamp *Snap on table lamp*	(Page 1)
Cue 2	**Henry** turns out main lights *Snap off brackets or pendant*	(Page 1)
Cue 3	**Katherine** serves casserole *Fade to Black-Out, then up to previous lighting*	(Page 10)
Cue 4	**Katherine** pulls out lamp flex *Flash, then Black-Out*	(Page 14)
Cue 5	Hoover sound dies down *Fade up to daylight. Fire lit*	(Page 15)
Cue 6	**Henry:** "We'll start tomorrow." *Fade to Black-Out, then up to artificial lighting*	(Page 20)
Cue 7	**Katherine:** "—a gardener." *Fade to spot on Katherine*	(Page 23)
Cue 8	As **Sam** sits on sofa *Fade up to bright daylight*	(Page 23)
Cue 9	**Sam** exits *Fade to Black-Out, then up to artificial lighting*	(Page 24)
Cue 10	**Henry** switches off main lights *Snap off artificial lighting*	(Page 29)
Cue 11	**Henry** switches on electric fire *Room lit up by warm glow from fire*	(Page 30)
Cue 12	**Henry** switches on main lights *Snap on full artificial lighting*	(Page 33)

ACT II. Night

To open: As close of previous Act

Cue 13	**Henry** sits on sofa *Fade to Black-Out, then up to previous lighting*	(Page 39)
Cue 14	**Sam** lies on sofa *Fade to Black-Out, then up to daylight*	(Page 50)
Cue 15	**Katherine:** "I don't know." *Fade to Black-Out, then up to full artificial lighting*	(Page 57)

EFFECTS PLOT

ACT I

Cue 1	**As Curtain rises** *Pop music from radiogram*	(Page 1)
Cue 2	**Katherine** stops radio *Music off*	(Page 2)
Cue 3	**Henry** puts on record *Elvis Presley music*	(Page 5)
Cue 4	**Record:** Elvis singing *Doorbell rings*	(Page 5)
Cue 5	**Katherine** enters with bath *Doorbell rings*	(Page 5)
Cue 6	**Katherine** stops record *Music off*	(Page 5)
Cue 7	**Katherine** pushes potty down stage *Doorbell rings*	(Page 5)
Cue 8	**Sam** enters *Sound of chopping from kitchen*	(Page 5)
Cue 9	**Sam:** ". . . cut your balls off, feller?" *Telephone rings*	(Page 8)
Cue 10	**Henry** puts on record *Music—slow foxtrot*	(Page 13)
Cue 11	**Katherine** stops record *Music off*	(Page 13)
Cue 12	**Katherine:** ". . . bring them all home." *Doorbell rings*	(Page 13)
Cue 13	**Katherine** and **Henry** murmur behind sofa *Doorbell rings*	(Page 14)
Cue 14	As Lights come up *Doorbell rings*	(Page 15)
Cue 15	**Katherine:** "—married to an electrician." *Telephone rings*	(Page 16)
Cue 16	**Katherine** and **Sam** look at each other after unplugging Hoover *Telephone rings*	(Page 24)
Cue 17	**Henry** puts receiver down *Telephone rings*	(Page 28)
Cue 18	**Henry:** "—life in Belsize Park." *Alarm clock rings*	(Page 29)

ACT II